VISIBLE GODS

D. E. HARDING

# VISIBLE GODS

## A MODERN SOCRATIC DIALOGUE

D. E. Harding

"Some of the gods whom we honour are clearly visible."

Plato, *Laws.*

Published by The Shollond Trust

London

Published by The Shollond Trust
87B Cazenove Road
London N16 6BB
England

headexchange@gn.apc.org
www.headless.org

The Shollond Trust is a UK charity, reg. no 1059551
Copyright © The Shollond Trust 2016
Design and layout by rangsgraphics.com
ISBN 978-1-908774-01-9

The Shollond Trust

London

VISIBLE GODS

# Foreword

After Faber & Faber published his great book, *The Hierarchy of Heaven and Earth*, in 1952, Douglas Harding returned to practising architecture – very successfully – after a break of more than ten years. (It took Harding ten years to write *The Hierarchy*.) However, though Harding was now designing buildings again, he didn't give up writing – he didn't stop trying to share with the world his message about who we really are. In 1955 he finished *Visible Gods*, a deeply inspiring book that contains many ideas from *The Hierarchy*, but in an easier-to-read form. Harding did not succeed in publishing *Visible Gods*, so it is with delight that we do so now.

*Visible Gods* takes the form of an imaginary dialogue between Socrates and four fictitious modern-day characters. Socrates' worldview is of a living cosmos with man only half-way up the hierarchy of all beings; above him reign suprahuman beings of great majesty and power – the visible gods. The moderns with whom Socrates converses disdain his ancient Greek cosmos as primitive and false. Yet as Socrates questions them in typically ironic fashion about the discoveries of science, it's not at all clear that the scientists' view of "a dead universe populated here and there with rare accidents of life" is right. Indeed, the more the moderns argue their case, the more Socrates shows they are arguing his…

The challenge we moderns face is to put aside our 'commonsense' preconceptions about the universe and see – and accept – what science is telling us.

I met Douglas Harding in 1970. I first read the original, uncondensed *Hierarchy* in 1975 whilst staying with Douglas. I was profoundly inspired – it opened my eyes to a new world. Later in the same year I read *Visible Gods*. I must have written to Douglas about it, for here's part of a letter he sent me, dated November 12, 1975:

> I am so happy that V.G. is finding a reader! I must have a go myself, sometime. I have a strong sense of writing for future generations, but it is so good to have [a] little preview of how men may one day discover their cosmic meaning and identity, partly through writings like V.G.
>
> Judging by my own tendency to drop off, to return to the normal doze and stupor, our task will be, and is, anyhow, to keep waking up. I'm a maker of alarm clocks, I hope, for this purpose; hopefully set to go off at frequent intervals. Taking everything for granted, without astonishment, which means without thankfulness too, is such a pity.

*Visible Gods* is an alarm clock Douglas Harding set more than fifty years ago. It is now ringing.

Richard Lang,

# CONTENTS

# Characters

Socrates

Sir Hugo Canopus, late Astronomer Royal

Archdeacon Brown

Dr. Theodor Schmidt, late President of the International Association for Psychotherapy

Waldo Cowen, late Director of the Biological Institute, Chicago, and sometime Professor of Biochemistry in the University of Illinois

# ONE

Socrates: ...Though I admit it's not much like Homer's idea of Hades.

Brown: I should think not – just look at those stars!

Canopus: Well, we've argued the point all day long and hardly got any further. Shall we leave it for the moment, my dear Socrates, and agree to differ? You can't talk Cowen and me out of our idea that we've somehow been switched from our normal terrestrial set-up into another which is just as physical and secular, but whose dimensions of time and space don't happen to square with ours. (After all, it's not so very different here: this chair feels solid enough; the fire's nice and warm this frosty night; your good wine, Socrates, couldn't go down better; and the stars I can see out of your window look perfectly familiar, if brighter than usual.) The Archdeacon, on the other hand, sticks to his opinion that this place is a kind of supernatural anteroom where we wait about for our summons to the Last Judgment, though he doesn't rule out the possibility – more flattering for him than us – that he's dreaming it all, and will presently wake up in his parsonage in Surrey. As for Dr Schmidt, he keeps an open mind. What we're more or less agreed on is that our arrival here arose out of an experiment that didn't come off – or went off rather too well. It's a pity we can't remember quite what happened.

Brown: Well, I certainly remember saying it was madness to muck about with the electron like that. As if the H-bomb weren't enough! Perhaps our... disappearance (if you prefer that word) will teach a few of our back-room boys a lesson. But let's drop the subject and turn to something pleasanter. We may be displaced persons, but it's a tremendous consolation to find *you* with us – Socrates of all people!

Socrates: My dear friends, the catastrophe which dispatched you is a godsend for me. You couldn't be more welcome. It's over 23 centuries since I retired to this place (whatever you choose to call it) and all this time knowledge has been piling up in your world. I've heard plenty about your wonderful discoveries – and even picked up some of the jargon – but understood little or nothing. Now I have the lucky chance, by becoming your pupil, of learning from the best and latest masters. Only I beg you to be patient with my ignorance, remembering that I am in effect a child who is younger than you by millenniums.

Canopus: You're too modest Socrates. It is we who are privileged to meet *you*, the great pioneer. And, besides underestimating yourself, you overestimate us. For one thing – though I'm an astronomer, and really know nothing about philosophy and art and ethics – I doubt whether there's been any great or certain progress in these things since your day. What do you think Archdeacon?

Brown: Well, philosophers still seem to be asking the kind of questions you used to ask, Socrates, or – more often – have given up trying to answer them. And certainly if we moderns have bettered the Odyssey or the Parthenon or the Hermes of Praxiteles, I've still to hear about it. As for wisdom and virtue, I doubt – to put it mildly – whether the proportion of good men to bad and of wise to foolish is any greater now than it was in the Athens of Pericles. In fact, many would say we've gone back. For instance in politics and religion...

Socrates: But your science?

Canopus: I was coming to that, Socrates. In pure and applied science – in our knowledge of the world, and in our use of that knowledge to control the world...

Socrates: The Z-bomb?

Canopus: Well, leave aside the question of control. At any rate in our *knowledge* of the universe about us there has, particularly during recent centuries, been a huge increase. This is certainly not because we're cleverer than you, Socrates, but because we've hit on methods of observation and verification, and techniques of mathematical analysis, which have made for very rapid accumulation of knowledge. The credit doesn't belong to us as individuals but rather to our increasing division of labour, and to our giving up speculation for empiricism, so that even a quite stupid specialist can, by starting where his teachers leave off, push a little further into the unknown. Yes, my dear Socrates, of one thing we moderns may reasonably be proud, and that's our discovery – however incomplete – of what the world is really like.

Socrates: This is wonderful news! To know the universe – however incompletely – by Zeus, what an achievement! And I, poor ignoramus, never got anywhere near to knowing that tiny fragment of it called man! Well, like a good child starting school, I'm ready to forget the tales of the nursery and learn the wisdom of men. Let me give you an instance. Many of us in ancient Greece liked to think of the universe as full of life and divinity, of the sun and stars as visible gods, and of the blue sky as the heaven of the blessed. We looked up into heavens at once theological and astronomical, and the further from us they were the more lively and divine they were likely to be. Physical height went with spiritual status. All childish imaginings which – so they tell me – are now completely disproved. You distinguished gentlemen have the facts, and I shall let no such fancies stand in their way.

Canopus: In your time, Socrates, such beliefs were plausible enough. But I'm afraid anyone who held them nowadays would invite – not, it's true, a dose of hemlock, but something quite bad enough – psychological treatment from Dr. Schmidt here – private treatment if he were rolling in money, institutional if he weren't.

Schmidt: Sir Hugo likes to have his little dig at us.

Socrates: To speak plainly, a man holding such opinions would be thought mad?

Schmidt: Let's say eccentric, though probably quite harmless; anyhow, a most interesting case. I remember a patient of mine...

Canopus: If I may interrupt, Dr. Schmidt, I think – before we go any further – we ought to give Socrates some rough idea of the universe we moderns find ourselves in.

Socrates: I should be very grateful, Sir Hugo. But don't forget I'm a baby in these things. Come down off your professional high horse and be as chatty and informal as you can, otherwise I'll never understand you.

Canopus: Very well, then. Try to think of the Earth as a tiny spinning globe sweeping out yearly a great circle, a couple of hundred million miles wide, about the Sun, which is big enough to hold more than a million Earths, and made of very hot material – far too hot, I assure you, to support any form of life. The rest of the planets – Mercury, Venus, Mars, Jupiter, Saturn, and some others observed since your time, Socrates – move like the Earth, but at different speeds and in different orbits, round the Sun; and the whole collection we call the Solar System. But *collection's* hardly the word: it's a real whole, for not only did the planets doubtless come from the Sun in the first place – they've never left it. They're the Sun's own growth or development, the petals of a star that has burst into bloom. Or – to be more prosaic – think of this expanded star as an egg broken into a frying pan, with the Sun as the yolk and the planets as bubbles of various sizes in the white. Better still, imagine the bubbles swimming round and round the pan so swiftly that they become circles.

Socrates: You make the universe sound most appetizing!

Canopus: That's only the first course. You must now think of this huge rotating fried egg as no more than an almost invisible bubble in the white of another rotating fried egg called the Galaxy. To give you any true idea of the size of the Galaxy is almost impossible, but let me try. It contains many thousands of millions of stars comparable with our own, and the nearest of them is millions of millions of miles away. The centre of the whole revolving system is thousands of times more distant still.

Socrates: My head's swimming too!

Canopus: Now for the third course! Our Galaxy itself is only one of millions of visible galaxies or nebulae – to say nothing of those that no doubt lie beyond the range of our telescopes… In short, Socrates, our seemingly vast and central and all-important Earth is really an infinitesimal dust-grain, which happens at the moment to exist in an immense universe that is certainly neither made for the dust-grain's convenience nor likely to worry about the dust-grain's fate – to say nothing of the fate of men, who are this dust-grain's own dust. The human needle is quite lost in the cosmic haystack.

Socrates: And yet, as you've shown quite well, it's acutely aware of the haystack, and in that sense contains it. A curiously compressible haystack, I must say, or else a curiously capacious needle – and one which demonstrates that it has found rather than lost its bearings! It can only be your admirable modesty which makes you gloss over the fact.

Canopus: That's all very well, Socrates, from the needle's private point of view, the subjective one. But it's precisely this viewpoint that we scientists try to avoid. To the detached observer, living creatures in general, and conscious living creatures in particular, are the rarest things in the world and quite untypical.

Socrates: So this human needle looks at itself objectively, from a universal point of view – doesn't that make it far more remarkable still? Nor should I hold its rarity against it: after all, it's the rarest stone which is the most precious. And who would think, my dear Sir Hugo, of measuring your significance solely by your bulk or your commonness? A man's ability to entertain and weigh up this wonderful universe of stars and galaxies is surely at least as revealing as his ability to turn the scale at so many pounds. To me, at least, you are more interesting than all the lifeless worlds which, when they enter into your life, can scarcely escape its infection. And certainly you are ten thousand times more handsome – and that's not to be sniffed at either!

Canopus: Spare my blushes, Socrates. But no doubt, after allowance has been made for Socratic buttering up, there's a lot in what you say. The mind of one speck of this Earth-speck of ours can easily take a few million galaxies in its stride... However I didn't mean to suggest that, apart from our planet, there's no life at all in our universe. Mars possibly supports living creatures, and some of my friends think it certainly does. Venus is a more doubtful case. (To say – without going thoroughly into it – that *all* the 'evidence' for flying saucers *must* be rubbish is mere provincialism and lack of imagination, blind worship of the human parish pump.) The other planets of our system are almost certainly dead worlds. So are all the stars – as mere stars. But according to recent theories, many of them are likely to have developed into solar systems similar to our own – in which case some no doubt contain planets like our Earth, with all the conditions necessary for life. And where such conditions occur... But now I'm straying out of the astronomer's province into yours, Professor Cowen.

Cowen: Where the conditions of life are found – the right temperature and the right chemical ingredients – there, we believe, life will eventually be found also. It would follow that, though the universe which Sir Hugo has described is a vast desert of lifeless space, thinly dotted with equally lifeless condensations of matter, it does contain here and there many infinitesimal life-specks.

Socrates: Some of which may surpass our own?

Cowen: It would be odd if none did.

Socrates: I suppose the chances are that, to find the more accomplished – the more superhuman – of these life–specks, we should need to look further and further afield from our Earth-centre.

Cowen: I don't follow.

Socrates: The further you look the vaster and more embracing the heavenly objects you come across, and the more life they are likely to contain. And more life means more life to choose from. The realm of the nine planets is plainly not such promising country as the remoter realm of the stars – the hundreds of millions of stars of our own Galaxy, supporting goodness knows how many planets. Nor is this realm a millionth part as rich in celestial possibilities as the still remoter realm of the galaxies, with their unthinkable great star-population.

Canopus: That's true enough.

Socrates: Now I wonder if the more godlike of the creatures who live in these realms above could find some way of influencing men without their knowing it. What do you think, Dr. Schmidt?

Schmidt: Well, telepathy does occur. Minds have hidden ways of getting at one another.

Socrates: Unfortunately the distance between the stars is so great.

Schmidt: It seems that distance has nothing to do with it.

Socrates: Well, gentlemen, let me try to sum up what I've learned so far. It seems that – after all – a man may enjoy the thought, whenever he looks up into the starry sky, that he's not idly staring at a mere rubbish dump or cemetery, but at the many-storied home of beings who may so far excel him that they merit his reverence as divine. Indeed his thoughts of them may be in part their own work, and directly inspired.

You speak of these beings as if it were somehow to their *discredit* that their dwelling is on so grand – so truly celestial – a scale, but in my day the palace was the measure of the king. Do yours live in hovels? And it's not as if the universe's royal family were unaware of their palace, or lost in its endless corridors: on the contrary, they carry the whole thing in their royal heads.

But the palace, you inform me, is "a vast desert of lifeless space". What has it failed to do, or done, to earn from you such disparagement? By virtue of this despised empty space, all the wonders of Earth and heaven are freely presented to you, so that wherever you are there you find the whole, marvelously gathered up into a point. In fact it is *you* who, without it, are utterly empty. *It* is filled to overflowing, and you are filled, if at all, at its inexhaustible fountain. All you've told me goes to show that, so far from being mean and poor, this royal suite – and this miraculous union of expanse and concentration, of presence and omnipresence – is furnished with a splendour beyond description, and well deserves our awestruck admiration. What is this space, considered not in the abstract but as it actually comes to us – saturating and saturated with our mind, if no other – but Heaven itself? It is indeed a very comical mind that spends its time trying to sweep the universe clear of itself (thus doing quite the opposite thing), and then goes on to complain that the universe is mindless!

As for the design of these heavenly mansions, I find it strangely familiar. Apparently there's good reason, after all, for matching physical height and spiritual status. Distance lends more than enchantment.

In short, my friends, if I hadn't been told otherwise, I'd have said you were out to *defend* my ancient universe instead of shatter it!

# TWO

Socrates: But what puzzles me is how these heavenly mansions come to be inhabited. I take it that living creatures, having arrived in the universe from another and less material realm, seek out – or else find by accident – a solar system with a planet ripe for habitation, and found a colony there.

Cowen: Nothing of the sort, Socrates. The creatures are merely the inevitable product, the ripening, of the planet itself. The life of the Earth – we've every reason to believe – has gradually developed from the raw materials of its surface. I can't begin to do justice to the story now, but this is the gist of it: more and more complex parcels of matter arose – were cooked up, so to say, in the presence of warmth and moisture – till some of them began to show signs of life; and in the course of ages their progeny grew up, through more and more elaborate forms, into such creatures as fish, amphibians, reptiles, mammals, and men. Such, my dear Socrates, is our ancestry. We have sprung from the slime and not the heavens, from beasts and not gods. We aren't colonists or visitors upon the Earth, but elaborations of her substance, as truly her natural outgrowths as leaves on a tree.

Socrates: You're *quite* sure of that?

Cowen: I've never been more sure of anything. And the

same is doubtless true of any other planet which supports a population: the life is its own and no celestial invasion, a slow and natural development and not a sudden miracle.

Socrates: I'm afraid that for me, my dear Professor, the gradualness does nothing to reduce the mystery. I should find you just as surprising and admirable – whether you arose from the rock at the wave of a wand or took a hundred million years about it. But let that pass. Clearly I must learn this difficult lesson from you: that plants and animals and men haven't been planted or grafted or dropped upon the Earth, but are rather her living organs. But the souls of men – surely they have other and nobler origins?

Cowen: I don't quite know what you mean by a soul; as for a soul without a body, that seems to me nonsense. It's enough for me to observe man's structure and behaviour. And everything goes to show they derive from – are elaborations of – the structure and behaviour of his primitive human ancestors, and of their animal ancestors, and so back and back to the structure and behaviour of the simplest particles from which we've all sprung. I can find no break in the development from raw matter to man, no dividing line which might suggest supernatural interference, or the arrival of some ghostly invader called mind or soul. Nature has a certain continuity, and doesn't make leaps of that sort.

Socrates: And you, Dr. Schmidt, who are a professor of the soul: what do you think?

Schmidt: I'm a practical man, Socrates. I find that many of my patients are ill because they refuse to face their past – all of it, no matter how disreputable or primitive. To cut oneself off from one's individual and racial origins can amount to a kind of suicide. When I study a patient's troublesome experience, it often happens that I can't understand it – and so can't help him – until I link it with the experience of his ancestors. And remember: these ancestors extend right back into the world of the most primitive creatures. In fact, I'm quite unable to say where something like experience stops, and 'mere matter', without any rudiment of awareness of the world, begins. All the indications, so far as I can see, are against supernatural origins. I don't doubt our minds are derived from the same source as our bodies, namely the stuff of our planet.

Canopus: Which is ultimately the same stuff – electrons, protons, and such-like particles – as all the galaxies and stars and planets are made of.

Socrates: I take it that, mixed everywhere with these particles, are some which – divinely gifted – are the seeds of life.

Cowen: On the contrary, Socrates, we believe that the basic material of living things is no different from the basic material of dead ones. Given the right conditions, these primitive particles are *all* capable of organization into the highest living creatures, and even into Socrates himself!

Socrates: Fortunately most of them have other plans! Well, it's not for me to doubt my schoolmasters. But I'm bound to say that, so far from damping my enthusiasm for the universe, you've wonderfully inflamed it. You began by showing me that the world is spacious and splendid beyond all I'd childishly imagined. Then you drew a picture, not of empty and godforsaken heavens, but of a widespread life that is worthy of such housing: indeed you yourselves, though minute fractions, show a comprehension of the whole which I'm tempted to call superhuman. And now you've capped it all by telling me that this magnificent home of life is itself, with all its appointments – all the stuff of all the stars – potentially alive, sentient, human, and even divine. Though the actuality is rare the potentiality is universal. Henceforth I shall hold the meanest stick and stone – to say nothing of the Sun and stars – in reverence. The old philosopher had better reason than he knew for saying that the world is full of gods.

Now I see, gentlemen, that you were hardly serious when you talked of such a view – or something like it – as madness. Is it, I wonder, that you hate making a parade of your piety, or that you would use a kind of irony – such as I once tried my hand at – to draw your halting pupil on?

# THREE

Canopus: What a dear old optimist you are, Socrates! I only wish the picture were as pretty as you paint it. But fond wishes are one thing and cruel facts another. Lord knows we moderns have a lot to feel ashamed of, but at least we've dared to take the rose-tinted spectacles off our noses and look the universe in the face without flinching, in the harsh light of reality. You may think the sight is a heart-warming one: I don't. Planets and stars and galaxies aren't in fact alive, much less human or divine. However interesting their potentiality, it is worlds apart from their actuality.

Cowen: What exactly is potentiality, anyhow. Does the word in that context mean anything definite at all?

Canopus: I think the trouble, Socrates, is that we're conversing with you across a vast gulf of time. It's not easy, but I'd like to put over to you, if I could, some hint of the human situation as most men of education see it in the 20th century. By some accident this universe and galaxy and star – this nest of cosmic dice-boxes – has shaken out a pattern of particles called man: in the immense wastes of space-time something of the sort was bound to happen somewhere, sooner or later. But it will all come to the same thing in the end. The particles will jostle themselves back into normal futility soon enough. You've noticed how the bright rim of a cloud in the sky, or a coal in the grate, will now and again take on the shape of a man's face, with every feature clearly outlined. Well, man is like that. He has about as much reason for putting on airs in the universe as a fleck of foam for lording it over the seven seas. He's far from being, as you seem to think, at home among the stars; at least – if you want my opinion – the home-sweet-home you have to fight for your life in isn't a home, or even a prison, but a cockpit. Man is a stranger in a hostile world. Or, more accurately, in a world that *happens* to be against him: it's far too fat-headed to be against him *intentionally.*

Socrates: But my dear fellow, the Professor here has scarcely finished pulling me up for talking like that about man as a rank outsider, a stranger wandering in an alien country! Nonsense (I was told): he is every bit as much the world's natural offshoot as a leaf is the tree's. Are you now saying I was right after all? Which of you am I to believe? What is the modern view? For myself, in my day I never found myself *fighting* the sunlight that warmed me, or the air I breathed, or the water I drank, or the animals and plants I ate, or even the men who clothed and housed me. Quite the contrary: the whole world might have been designed for my sole edification and delight! How horribly it must have changed since then!

Canopus: I'm not denying there've been some fortunate accidents – of which man is one.

Socrates: And what an accident! By heavens, it was a fortunate throw of the dice – such a masterpiece of charm and intelligence as yourself, and the variegated life-stories of all five of us here, and dear Athens, and the immense ferment of human history from Homer down to the Z-bomb, and the sustained improbability of all life and the worlds that serve life – and everything in due sequence! What a run of luck! It's just as if all things that ever lived spent all their time tossing coins, getting nothing but heads...

Brown: ...and would instantly vanish if anyone threw a tail! Perhaps the Z-bomb was just that!

Socrates: Don't you think we've turned out rather well, Archdeacon, all things considered? Aren't you pleased with us? We may be excused a few shortcomings, and even the odd Z-bomb, it seems. Why, the continued existence of a paltry grain of sand for a split second amounts to the achievement of the almost impossible, and calls for wonder and rejoicing and universal celebrations! Or so, in my antiquated simplicity, I should have thought. And what shall we say of our dear Astronomer Royal – this fortuitous commotion of particles that goes round blandly introducing itself as such? What an engaging spectacle it is: a good-looking, self-critical, distinguished, humourous, urbane, intellectual, moral, universe-probing – but alas accidental – rough-and-tumble of atoms! If this is possible,

I should like to know what isn't! To swallow such a camel, yet strain at the gnat of a skyful of gods, is very curious.

Brown: The miracles of religion are incredible – so *this* is the sort of thing we believe before breakfast!

Socrates: To tell you the honest truth, Sir Hugo, I find your tale of woe distinctly encouraging. If you yourself – to go no further afield – are an instance of what this old gambler of a universe can toss off *by accident,* it has surely earned from you a modicum of respect and even admiration, instead of some of the hard names you've been calling it. And just think what it couldn't do if ever it got around to doing it *intentionally!*

Canopus: I think we can rule out that possibility, Socrates!

Socrates: But can we? If such glorious deeds have already been performed by blind chance, why not one day this crowning glory? If the universe has done so much of the job so well by accident, what's to prevent it finishing the job and becoming an intentional universe – oh of course by accident!

Canopus: It's not a lot of use guessing what the universe *might* do. What it *does* is the point. And I fail to find any intention in what it does.

Socrates: My dear sir, you don't look very far! It does *you,* and you seem to be positively bursting with intention! Myself also. And at any rate *this* part of the dice-game – the part which so intentionally announces that it is Socrates – firmly intends itself: you have its own word for it. What's more, it firmly intends the Canopus part of the game, and the Cowen and Brown and Schmidt parts, and in fact the whole accidental bag of tricks! And the same, unless I'm much mistaken, is true of you, and of all intelligent beings in the universe who aren't actually on the point of committing suicide.

Brown: Or touching off Z-bombs.

Socrates: How your universe can be so steeped in intention, yet remain merely accidental, is a puzzle too deep for me. But at least it is clear that, however the dice-game-without-a-player – *if* that's what it is – may have started off, it has now in some places begun to play itself in earnest. That part of the game we are really qualified to talk about – namely ourselves, our own terrestrial and solar part of it – is waking up and taking the liveliest interest in itself and all the world.

# FOUR

Canopus: It all sounds wonderful, Socrates. The universe has certainly found a keen apologist – I only wish I could follow him! But I do admire your spirit. By all means let's look on the brighter side: the last thing I want to do is to belittle man. He's certainly not without his brief glory, which (in my opinion) is to face cheerfully his ultimate insignificance. As far as my information goes, the universe – and, in particular, this vast Catherine wheel of a galaxy which has absentmindedly worked him out of its system – is itself quite heartless and brainless. But to know this and not give in, to squeeze some momentary drops of value out of the inane, to cock a snook at fate, and above all to keep a sense of humour in a grim-faced universe – this is to be a *man*. Though the universe will certainly destroy him, it needn't defeat him. He doesn't have to cringe and crawl before the thing, or heap compliments on it, even if he is its waste-product or oversight. At least he can be a *noble* accident.

Socrates: Spoken like a man, Sir Hugo! You'd inspire the most faint-hearted to face the worst bravely and say goodbye to all self-deception. But what, precisely, *is* the worst? I'm afraid this confused old brain of mine creaks along very slowly, a long way behind yours.

Canopus: How do you mean?

Socrates: Do you mind if I lower the tone of our conversation for a moment and talk about something quite trivial – coming down with a bump from the galaxies to the level of a humble plant? A certain man from the East, an excitable little Indian merchant I ran into one day in the marketplace in Athens, told me the story – if you can call it that. It seems this plant – a kind of cactus – had grown in his garden for ten years or more, putting forth any number of spiked and bloated leaves, but in all that time never the hint of a flower. The wretched vegetable was worse than a weed: it was a positive menace and eyesore. I can't think why he didn't dig it up and have done with it – unless he suspected it was too bad to be true, and likely at any time to show a better side to its nature, since it couldn't show a worse one. Anyhow, it was as well he waited. Walking in his garden one moonlit night, he came on a new and exquisite smell. It was from the cactus. There out of the dirt-coloured leaves and thorns rose a wonderful flower bigger than a man's hand, all milky white and shining in the light of the moon; and the petals (so he told me) seemed to be actually trembling with the surprise and thrill of their own life. Next morning it had withered away, and the plant never flowered again... Well, that's all. Not a very exciting tale, I'm afraid, but the incident had evidently made a deep impression on my rather emotional Indian friend. Apparently his cactus plant had become to him a precious symbol, a key to many locked doors. I think he must have infected my more matter-of-fact mind with just a little of his enthusiasm, seeing that I remember him and his story as if he had told it yesterday.

Canopus: A charming miniature! I'm sure we shall all be most intrigued to hear what exactly it has to do with our picture of the universe.

Socrates: That will come out – with your help. I'd like, if I may, to ask a few questions. Professor Cowen, you're an expert in these things. Would you call my friend's cactus a *flowering* plant?

Cowen: Why of course.

Socrates: And it would still be a *flowering* plant, and not the other sort, never mind how small and brief its flower and how big and long-lived its leaves?

Cowen: Naturally.

Socrates: One swallow doesn't make a summer, you know.

Cowen. I've heard of a swallow turning up at the wrong time and place, but never of a flower turning up on the wrong plant. Your cactus is a *flowering* plant from start to finish, and whether you happen to catch it actually in bloom or not makes no odds at all. You have to take the life-history *as a whole,* and the flower episode – no matter how brief – is just about the most revealing part of it.

Socrates: And you stick to this rule throughout nature?

When you want to classify a specimen you look mainly to its most developed stage – without, of course, ignoring the others?

Cowen: Precisely. For instance, you must know that there are creatures which, having spent almost all their lives pretending to be mere worms, come out briefly at the end in their true colours, as splendid winged insects. And that's how we classify them.

Socrates: You're quite sure that you're not looking at them through rose-tinted spectacles, and that in the harsh light of reality they wouldn't be seen as mere grubs after all?

Cowen: Isn't that an unnecessary question?

Socrates: Well, we've had a plant and an animal. Now what about a man? I hope you won't feel embarrassed, Sir Hugo, if I seem to be fishing, and ask you what you think of me. Do you feel as if you're talking to a well-conducted cloud of particles, or a foetus that's got above itself, or a perambulating food-tube? Or, on the contrary, to a partially intelligent person named Socrates, son of Phaerenete the midwife? In other words, do you take me at my best – such as it is – or at something much less than that.

Canopus: My dear fellow, how do I *seem* to be taking you?

Cowen: I must say, Socrates, I don't see the point of all

these rhetorical questions.

Brown: Surely it's plain what Socrates has got up his sleeve.

Socrates: Oh no, Archdeacon! My task – my divinely appointed mission, as I like to think – is to persuade *others* to bring out what, unknown to them, is up *their* sleeves: mine were shaken empty long ago. If what I'm going to produce turns out to be unwelcome, you my friends are responsible for it. Don't blame me!

Cowen: Suppose we decide that after we've heard what it is.

Socrates: It's this: either you, Professor Cowen, or you, Sir Hugo, are talking rubbish. Oh not seriously – I imagine – but just having a little game with me for my own good. Presumably I have to find out which of you it is.

Canopus: I'm quite innocent of any such stratagem, and I could swear Cowen is too.

Brown: And I can add, Socrates, that they've only been voicing the so-called common sense of our age. If there are wild inconsistencies in it – and, heaven help us, it looks as though there are – we never notice them.

Cowen: Do stop being so elaborately mysterious, Socrates.

Socrates: Surely the issue is quite plain: which of you am I to believe, since it's impossible to believe both? How am I to take things – at their best with the Professor, or at their worst with Sir Hugo? Shall I recognize achievement or ignore it? One thing I can't do, namely treat the very big and very little things (such as galaxies and suns and particles, with the space that holds them all) on one principle, looking always on the dark or undeveloped side, and treat the medium-sized things (such as plants and animals and men) on the opposite principle, looking always on the bright or developed side. I have to choose which rule to go by and then stick to it, whatever happens to be the size of the object I'm examining. Well, which shall it be?

Brown: Supposing you tell us, Socrates.

Socrates: At my age, gentlemen, I find long abstract arguments rather a strain. Forgive me, therefore, if I hark back to my Indian's plant. It seems you require me to consider two versions of it.

The first version runs something like this. Our vast old cactus of a world has at last broken out into a tiny human flower, and what an odd one it is! Head in the air, it looks down its long stem at the cactus, and does its best to forget that there *is* a stem. It never stops congratulating itself for being all flower, and despising the cactus for being all leaves and thorns and roots – a poor flowerless vegetable. As if this were not enough, it actually declares a kind of holy war upon the plant – meanwhile taking good care to draw in secret every drop of its nourishment, its substance, its very life and being, and of course all its ammunition, from the enemy. "These repulsive leaves and vicious-looking spikes," it says to itself, "are the essential cactus, which I, the brief but beautiful flower, hereby repudiate and challenge. See how immensely superior I am in every way, with my delicious perfume, my delicate milkwhite petals all a-tremble with the joy of living! I'm the noble accident, the fantastic anomaly, the perfect clue to what the plant is *not* like!

Brown: It's just as well this cock-eyed human blossom only *imagines* it's the cut flower of the universe!

Socrates: Now let's try version number two. The flower sees the plant as essentially a flower-producing plant, and sees itself as essentially a plant-produced flower – a demonstration of what kind of plant it is. The flower is its own constant reminder of the real nature of that unpleasant confusion of leaves and prickles down there. Very properly it holds its head high: that's its function. It thinks the devil of a lot of itself, but still more of the vegetable that can come to such a head as itself. Willingly it gives credit for its life and loveliness and perfume to the whole, leaves and thorns and roots and all. Indeed it has a great tenderness and respect for them, seeing that their lowly earthiness is the inescapable condition of its own lofty achievement. For unless the root were content to be a sordid thing hidden in darkness, and the leaves to be mere unexciting leaves, the flower could never be the magnificent thing it is, or anything at all.

Well, Sir Hugo, take your pick. Which will you have, this flower or the other?

Canopus: You don't give me much choice, do you? And unfortunately it looks as if I can't get out of it by accusing you of cheating, either. I should like to have told you that flowers happen to be more dependent upon plants than plants and animals and men upon the universe, but obviously they are *less* dependent. For the flower relies on outside sun and air and insects besides its own stem and leaves and root, whereas of course every creature relies wholly and solely on the universe. In short, my dear Socrates, I'm bound to admit you've understated rather than overstated your case. And yet...

Socrates: And so our conclusion seems inevitable, doesn't it? Earth and the starry heavens are much more than a man's home – more even than his stem and leaves and root. And he is much more than their cherished tenant – more even than the flower by which they are chiefly to be judged. Not even Aspasia could find words for the intimacy of their union.

# FIVE

Canopus: Well, Socrates, this will take some time to chew over. But you've certainly started me wondering whether I've not been looking at the world through tinted spectacles after all – only grey instead of pink ones.

Socrates: Do yourself justice, Sir Hugo. You only put them on for certain occasions, I notice. You're much too decent a fellow to live down to your beliefs, most of the time. Look at the cheerful kindness you've been showing me all along, in spite of my infuriating conversational habits – past curing now, I'm afraid. If I'm really a deceitful smoke-screen of particles, you generously overlook the fact. And I bet you never walked into a shop and asked for a packet of ultimate particles – or even seeds – which might one day assume the pattern of pumpkins. You asked quite simply for pumpkin seeds, and in due course pointed out the *pumpkins* coming up in your garden, long before the first bud showed itself. You just can't help seeing the fruit in the seed, the butterfly in the caterpillar, the man in the machinery of his body. In short, ninety-nine hundredths of the time you don't dream of taking your own grey-spectacled principles seriously, and you'd be a terrible creature if you did! So much the better for you, and so much the worse for them.

Canopus: But when it comes to the universe, the morbid side of me comes out! I should *like* to believe in your comfortable universe, Socrates.

Socrates: It's as if your head made it a point of honour to contradict your heart – a most unhealthy condition, I'd have thought.

Brown: And unreasonable too. After all, isn't the heart as genuine an organ or sample of the universe as the head is, and aren't both together better evidence than either by itself? The cactus flower repudiating the root is silly enough, but one of its petals repudiating another is too much! But if our current belief in a dead and meaningless universe is heart-chilling, it is also convenient. It suits our book to live in a world we can fight, desecrate, blow up, and generally misbehave in without a twinge of conscience. Natural piety is dreadfully cramping. .

Cowen: It certainly is, Archdeacon. That's one reason why I've not much time for it. Socrates' attitude strikes me as essentially religious and mystical – not to say obscurantist – the sort that has always stood in the way of genuine science, which is only, after all, common sense tidied up a bit. In my opinion, Canopus, you've just let him hypnotize you with his slick talk and pretty stories about flowers. In any case I can't for the life of me see what all the fuss is about. It's beyond question that the world ultimately consists of particles, or waves, or something of the sort, and that they are capable of weaving some very interesting patterns which nobody intended or foresaw. Well, the scientist doesn't sit down in front of the patterns, saying his prayers to them or making admiring noises. He does his best to *explain* them by analyzing them as thoroughly as possible, down to their ultimate constituents.

Socrates: Admirable! There's only one thing that's troubling me. What *are* these particles, or waves, or something of the sort? I'd like to get a really clear idea of them.

Canopus: Impossible, my dear Socrates! They're by nature invisible, and what they are intrinsically no-one knows – or can know, it would seem. Even their behaviour is excessively mysterious.

Socrates: You were saying, Professor Cowen, that the world doesn't call for admiration so much as explanation, which in the last resort only its ultimate ingredients can supply. Or rather, which they *can't* supply, because (Sir Hugo points out) they are unfortunately inscrutable, and keep their precious information under their hats. All the mysteries of mind and values, of life and matter, are to be explained in terms of these ultimate constituents; but to explain the mysterious by the incomprehensible sounds a little queer to me. As for the universe which calls for such a programme, it appears determined to catch us out. We have the choice of the illusory or the unknowable. What is such a world but an enormous confidence trick?

Brown: You may be sure Professor Cowen doesn't really think that. To be a scientist is to trust nature, and have unqualified faith in her intelligibility and self-consistency.

Cowen: I'm quite capable of looking after myself, thank you Archdeacon. It's hard enough – perhaps impossible – to explain to Socrates what science is up to, without your assistance.

Socrates: You've taken on a dull pupil, Professor. I'm trying to comprehend you, and failing horribly. When *I* seek an explanation of life in terms of the things we can all see, and even understand in part, I'm an obscurantist; but when *you* seek an explanation in terms of the particles no-one can see or understand, you're the champion of common sense! *You,* the sceptic, believe in electrons that can accidentally make a mind; *I,* the credulous fellow, only postulate a mind that can deliberately make electrons! *You,* whose life-work is founded on simple faith in nature's self-consistency and transparency to mind, are free from religious prejudices; *I,* who don't yet know what to make of nature, am full of them! In all this, it's *you* who are the hard-headed realist, and *I* who am the wooly-minded mystic!

Well, I mustn't forget that we are also master and pupil, and most of the lesson is still to come.

# SIX

Socrates: Meantime, there's a question I'd particularly like to ask. How is it that one collection of those particles happens to make up some contemptible stone or star, and another collection Professor Cowen? Who or what wakes the brilliant life and mind in the one and leaves them sleeping in the other?

Cowen: Well, I'll tell you one thing that makes a difference: a man's an immense community of primitive living things called cells, and a stone isn't.

Socrates: Do you really mean to say, Professor, that you – so obviously your delightfully unique self and no other – are in fact a pack of wild animals? That'll take a lot of swallowing!

Cowen: The obvious is a polite name for the superficial. Beware first impressions, my friend: they never tell the whole story. It's the scale of the object that fools you. Magnify it, and the one is myriads of living things; diminish it, and they are one living thing.

Socrates: Wonder of wonders! But my dear Professor, how can *any* number of wild beasts make even the most miserable human being – to say nothing of such a splendid one as yourself?

Cowen: Everything depends on the organization, the patterning in time and space, of the basic components.

Whether you agree or not, Socrates, we have the greatest contempt for speculative or mystical or supernatural explanations – which anyhow explain nothing – but content ourselves with observing and describing what happens, making do with a minimum of theory. And our observations justify our saying that particles when arranged in certain patterns comprise atoms, and these when arranged in certain patterns comprise molecules, and these when arranged in certain patterns comprise living cells, and these when arranged in certain patterns comprise intelligent men. Now we happen to find, at each new level in this structure of wholes and parts, new goings-on and new qualities we can't find at the level below. Thus a man is a very different story from one of his cells, and the cell a very different story from one of its molecules, and so on.

In general, Socrates, where you have a closely integrated group of units of one level – units which differ in form and function, and whose mutual relations are complex enough – there you have a *new* whole, a unit of the next level of organization, emerging; and, with it, some novel characteristics. You can say if you like that it's the specialization of the parts that does the trick.

Socrates: What I think you sometimes call their division of labour?

Cowen: That's the general idea.

Socrates: Well now, are you moderns quite sure this wonderful series stops short at the level of man, so that he – with the similar inhabitants of other planets – is the crown of the hierarchy? Apparently you aren't, seeing that you go in for Doctors of Divinity. What a good thing we have one of them here to clear the point up.

Brown: Immeasurably above all, there is God, omnipresent, omniscient, omnipotent.

Socrates: So that we have, at the top of the scale, the God who is present everywhere; in the middle, the man who is present in a human body; at the bottom, the particle that is present nowhere to speak of, that is practically an absentee. And between the middle and the bottom of the scale such intermediate stages as the cell, the molecule, and the atom, which are present in progressively smaller factions of the world. Am I right?

Brown: Yes.

Socrates: In other words, the vast gap between man and his minutest particles is neatly closed by a descending series of increasingly subhuman parts. Now from what you've told me about nature's continuity, I must assume that the equally vast gap between man and the omnipresent God is equally well filled by an ascending series of increasingly superhuman wholes. Therefore when you deny the existence of the gods – or something of the kind – you are presumably pulling my leg.

Cowen: Your argument, Socrates, may impress the Archdeacon who believes in God, but hardly those of us who don't.

Socrates: Am I to take it, Professor, that you believe there exists above us, not only no God and no gods, but no higher kind of being at all? Does your ascending scale stop abruptly with man?

Cowen: Certainly it does – at least so far as our own corner of the universe is concerned.

Socrates: Tell me, how did science make this immensely important discovery?

Cowen: Scientists have enough to do without laboriously detecting the obvious.

Socrates: Obvious to you, perhaps. But not to me. To my mind this question is as hard as it is crucial. Have you never suspected that our attention may be naturally directed outwards to our equals and downwards to our inferiors, but only with difficulty upwards to our superiors? Of all the parts you know, how many are aware of the wholes they belong to? Yet the wholes exist. Again, are human society, and indeed the community of life, so lacking in division of labour, so little organized, that they in turn build no higher unit? Are they not, even for you, in fact the chief instance and exemplar of that integration which accounts (so you tell me) for man himself?

And in any case, when we find a natural scale or process

which seems to come to a sudden end in ourselves, oughtn't we to be especially sceptical and wary, lest we mistake the appearance – the view from our particular level and station in it – for the reality itself? Are we, alone among species, without our specific blind-spots, and in no danger of parochialism? Are we so perfect that it is useless to ask what more the universe could do?

I see you shake your heads, gentlemen. At the very least, then, this is a question that calls for very careful investigation. And so long as you casually dismiss it as a waste of time, I can't see how you can claim even to have *tried* sincerely to find out what the universe is like.

# SEVEN

Cowen: I give you my word, Socrates, that the bulkiest living things in the known universe are whales and certain giant trees that grow in my country, and the most intelligent are men. And if Sir Hugo has ever caught sight of a god or an angel through his telescope he's kept very quiet about it.

Socrates: Perhaps he wasn't looking for the right sort of thing. It's always very difficult to find something if you've no idea what it looks like.

Brown: There's a lot in what Socrates says. Who was it – some eminent Victorian scientist, I think – who said it was no good looking through your microscope till you knew roughly what you were after? The same could apply to the telescope.

Canopus: Well, I confess my knowledge of the anatomy of angels is so slight that I may have missed them. Cowen, isn't this more up your street?

Socrates: I beg you, gentlemen, not to make fun of me. Have pity on my ignorance, and adjust your instruction to your pupil by humouring him a little. Let's suppose this gap above us, this huge blank space in the order of things, isn't quite empty. Let's suppose there does exist, after all, a godlike creature which is as much larger than a man as he is larger than one of his cells. Now what would such a creature have to be like?

Cowen: I'm afraid our studies suggest that, in practice, there are natural limits to the bulk of a living creature, so that if it's too big it's unlikely to survive. Your giant, Socrates, is a mere dream.

Socrates: I've heard it said that wisdom sometimes comes in dreams; therefore dream with me a little longer, Professor... I take you to mean that this hypothetical monster is too big to live on Earth. Very well, then: let it take flight from its parent heavenly body and set up as a heavenly body on its own account. Couldn't it then be much bigger?

Canopus: I can answer that one. In fact, it would *have* to be very massive indeed, otherwise it could neither conveniently carry its own atmosphere and water-supply about nor keep a firm gravitational hold upon them. And without water, and without oxygen to breathe, and without something like an atmosphere to protect it from meteor showers and from dangerous kinds and quantities of radiation and from extremes of heat and cold, it could hardly live in the heavens. Your monster, Socrates, would be obliged to keep up a vast bulk, and wrap itself from head to toe in a thick blanket of air – rather a tall order, don't you think?

Socrates: Then it would be ready to go where it liked?

Canopus: Certainly not. It would have to keep fairly near to some star for warmth and energy. But then it would freeze to death on one flank and roast to death on the other, unless it kept turning itself about like meat on a spit. Even so, this dervish-like behaviour would be useless if the monster at any time absent-mindedly began falling into the star or falling away from it. The only practicable way of keeping a safe distance would be to go on flying round and round the star indefinitely.

Socrates: I suppose that would be a very difficult and exhausting job.

Canopus: Quite the contrary. Both movements – the spinning and the circling – would be the easiest thing in the world because, once begun, they would go on effortlessly and unceasingly; for it so happens that the physical laws of gravity and inertia would together take good care of our creature, wafting it along the right path.

Socrates: Another fortunate accident! What a bit of luck, this life-saving coincidence!

Canopus: In this convenient fashion, Socrates, your creature would save its skin. And make its skin: for we should expect it to live on sunlight... The only snag is that, if such a monster exists, no telescope has ever revealed it, and our speculation is somewhat futile. Though – to be fair – I admit I've never ransacked the skies for truant and overgrown animals!

Socrates: I'm an unhappy combination of a fanciful child and an ignorant old man, who begs your indulgence just a little longer. Professor Cowen, can you suggest what organs this perfectly ridiculous monster would need?

Cowen: For the life of me, sir, I can't imagine. But I can tell you some it *wouldn't* need. This remarkable figment of Sir Hugo's imagination sounds to me less like an astronomical Whale than an astronomical Cabbage, with the whole of its surface drinking in solar energy. You have my word for it that wings – not to mention hooves, fins, tentacles, claws, flippers, hands, feet – would in the sky be deformities fit only for a heavenly comic turn, and even a head would be absurdly out of place. As for streaming hair, and a pair of ruby lips, and two rows of gleaming white teeth, and a stomach and bowels and an anus – what would they be for, except an astronomical joke? But the whole thing's an astronomical joke anyhow – and on us too!

Socrates: God forbid I should show such disrespect!... Well, we seem to be left with some rounded body, lacking any limbs or marked features. But our creature could still find use, I suppose, for organs of sense.

Canopus: The heavenly spaces aren't noisy or scented or tasty: here tongue and nose and ears would be quite silly. But eyes your creature certainly could do with – eyes scattered all over its surface, preferably.

Brown: Like Ezekiel's wheels in the sky.

Socrates: What I'm wondering is how this lonely sky-dweller would pass the time, supposing he had any wits at all.

Canopus: The only thing I can suggest, as a remedy for boredom, is that he takes up star-gazing for a hobby. There's a lot to be said for it.

Socrates: What then?

Canopus: Well, if we must go on dreaming, let's make the most of it and enjoy ourselves! Our monster, now we've generously equipped him with binocular – or more than binocular – vision, could amuse himself by learning to see all the nearer heavenly bodies in their proper places instead of as mere dots on the firmament; in time he might succeed in judging the true sizes and distances and motions of them all. He could awake to his own behaviour, so that all his spinning and circling about his star became in the end perfectly deliberate and calculated. (After all, the skies have served as our own superbly fitted schoolroom and laboratory; and a creature that has made them his home has at least the opportunity of equaling our mathematics and astronomy.) To be as adapted to the celestial environment as men are to the terrestrial, he would need to grow huge eyes capable of seeing much further into space than we can, and sense organs we lack altogether. He would be sensitive to radiations we never feel, though they rain on us from the sky all the while. In many ways he would be well placed and constituted for leading a superhuman life. Indeed our celestial Cabbage is beginning to look more like an Angel – though a secular and pot-bellied one! I'm beginning to feel quite sorry, my dear Socrates, that he's only a dream.

Socrates: Then perhaps we should consider the possibility of other godlike beings, creatures wholly unlike ourselves, independent of solar rays, and with senses and modes of thought we can't conceive.

Canopus: No thank you! That would be an extreme of unprofitable guesswork which I, for one, won't run to. At least we've relied – up to now – on what we know, namely the pattern of earthly life, and changed it only so far as celestial circumstances seem to require.

Socrates: Gentlemen, I'm immensely grateful to you for explaining what kind of object we should look for when in search of a visible god. And I think we're agreed it's useless to seek a thing unless one has *some* notion of what it may be like.

Canopus: My dear chap, you're wasting your thanks, for your precious sky-giant is necessarily invisible. Even if he does live up there, playing ring-a-ring-a-roses round some star, he's much too far off for us to see even with our best instruments. And surely it's dawned on you that, even if we could see him through some telescope not yet invented, his size and shape and mass and behaviour and chemical composition would all – if our design for him is anything like right – so resemble those of a planet that we should simply take him for one, and be none the wiser.

Socrates: Well then, let's try again, and suppose our monster is unlucky enough to find himself in some remote part of the heavens without a convenient star at whose fires he can warm himself. How could he manage to live in such conditions?

Canopus: Do I have to answer that? Well, all I can say is: if you can't *find* what you need for survival the only thing is to *be* it. If we stick to our rule of taking life as we know it, and making the minimum alteration needed for an independent heavenly existence, then I suppose your starless monster must itself incorporate a starlike source of energy – a large central mass of intensely hot material, to maintain the smaller and cooler peripheral body we've already described.

Socrates: In which case you couldn't tell it from a star?

Canopus: Exactly. And in all our romancing we've made no progress at all!

Socrates: Except to discover that if the heavens contain any living bodies at all, they are likely (to all intents and purposes) to be planets and stars; and that many a star shining away there in the sky, my dear Astronomer Royal, may quite well be a visible god, a self-contained and self-supporting sky-creature, just as you've described him!

Canopus: It isn't *impossible*, I admit. But seriously...

Socrates: Doesn't it begin to look, Sir Hugo, as if our

suspicions of human bias may have been perfectly justified, and the scale of creatures may not, after all, come to a full stop with man?

As for those of us who, with the Archdeacon, believe in God, we've already seen that, without superhuman beings of some sort, there's a huge and inexplicable gap in the order of things. To fill it, we needed vast creatures – beings intermediate between God who is present everywhere and man who is present in a mere human body – and what could these creatures have been, after all, but heavenly bodies? Well, what have we found, so far? It looks as though, while seeking a round peg to fit our round hole, we may have come upon a universe full of them, and indeed very little else!

More and more I suspect that, under the cunning pretence of destroying the antique star gods – which I confess I often doubted – you are in fact bent on proving them to me over and over again, replacing my childish wavering faith with your grown-up science of the divine.

# EIGHT

Cowen: I've been listening to all this with mounting astonishment – not to say irritation. My dear Canopus, you really have let Socrates and your imagination run away with you. And your trouble, Socrates, is that you're still governed by ancient ways of thought, in spite of all the bits and pieces of information you've managed to pick up here. You haven't the remotest idea of the nature of life as we moderns see it.

Socrates: Ah, that's what I want to learn so much! What is Life?

Cowen: The point is there's no such thing. We no longer talk that way. There's only an observed kind of very elaborate behaviour, displayed by an observed kind of very elaborate physical organization, which for convenience we call living or vital: the adjective is a useful piece of shorthand, whereas the noun – Life – is a useless piece of verbiage. We no more need a Principle of Life to brood over living things than a Principle of Asininity to brood over silly fools.

Socrates: Please forgive this silly fool's mistake about the noun, and explain the adjective. What kind of organization and behaviour do you describe as living?

Cowen: We take things as we find them. And when we find a collection of dead (or rather, inert) particles organized into an irritable lump of jelly-like stuff, and the whole lump is always adjusting itself to a changing world in such a way as to keep its characteristic form and structure, taking in nourishment and getting rid of waste, and growing, and reproducing its kind, then – for brevity – we say it's alive.

Socrates: All living things are made up of nothing but this remarkable jelly?

Cowen: No. I was coming to that. Various essential parts of an animal – and this is particularly true of the bigger and less primitive ones – consist of substances which are not in themselves alive. But such 'dead' parts may be more vital than 'living' ones. Thus a man can make do with one lung and half a gut and no limbs at all, but not without a bloodstream; and the greater part of his life-blood is as dead as can be. And let me add that, if the river Ilissus wasn't made alive by our dear Socrates and his Phaedrus paddling in it, neither was the fluid in their veins made alive by the corpuscles floating in it. Which all goes to show how tricky the adjective *alive* is – to say nothing of the noun *Life*.

Socrates: Well, if ever I *felt* full of life, Professor, it was on that happy occasion long ago, when I sat with my friend by the stream and we talked of the blessed gods in the sky. But I see your difficulty, and how it won't do to argue from the living whole to a living part, or (for that matter) from the dead part to a dead whole. Evidently what is dead at one level of organization may be full of life at another, and at once dead and alive: you've made it clear that all depends on whether you're looking at the parts one by one, or at the living whole. But at least you know a living whole when you see it.

Cowen: I'm not so sure I do.

Socrates: Well, take the cells you were speaking about. You talked of them as living wholes, I think?

Cowen: They are and they aren't. A cell in Socrates' body, taken by itself, is a little animal with distinct boundaries; its birthday and moment of death aren't his; it picks up its living from the interior stream that flows by, and voids into it. And certainly it never suspects the existence of Socrates, or credits itself with serving his purposes, or has any idea of the connection between its own behaviour and his.

Socrates: What a pity! A Socrates-cell and a Phaedrus-cell sitting on the bank of some interior Ilissus of mine, with their tiny feet dangling in its waters, and talking about the blessed god Socrates in whom they live and move and have their being – talking about him instead of getting on with their public duties towards him – now there's a delightful thought! At least it's not impiety, but merely their shocking ignorance, which prevents the little wretches from recognizing their master! But I interrupt you, Professor.

Cowen: I was trying to explain how, in one sense, a cell in the human body is a separate living creature. On the other hand, the only way to understand its history and anatomy and physiology is to look on it, not as a separate creature at all, but as a highly specialized part of a higher living whole – as an organ (so to speak) rather than an organism.

Socrates: I notice you kindly refer to Socrates himself – this walking menagerie or city-on-legs – as a living whole.

Cowen: Again, he is and he isn't. It is a question of terms. If by a *whole* man you mean one who is self-contained and lacking in none of the essentials of life, then you can scarcely leave out the air in his lungs and the saliva in his mouth and the food in his stomach and the chyme in his guts. At least I should like someone to point out where they cease to be environment and become organism. And, if these are included in the whole of him why not the tools without which he would starve to death and the clothes without which he would freeze to death? After all he is, biologically speaking, far more dependent on his shoes than his toenails, and upon his good 'false' teeth than his bad 'real' ones; aren't they then his members, though of a quite different order?

Socrates: Yet you never bled when a man tore your coat, or laughed when he tickled you in the boat-ribs, or ached in all six legs when you sat too long in a chair. It doesn't take a surgeon to disarm you. You weren't literally born with a silver spoon in your mouth; and if the spoon you later acquired was a kind of growth at the end of your arm, then it was amputated with unusual ease, and a knife or a fork or a hammer or a pen grown in its place.

Canopus: Socrates is quite right. Now it's you, Cowen, who ought to keep a check on himself!

Cowen: I'm quite capable of looking after myself, thank you. I was about to explain to Socrates that it's precisely this detachability and interchangeability, and the many other qualities which clearly distinguish the tool from the organ it prolongs, which make it so effective a part of the whole man. He can incorporate and then discard any limb-ending he fancies because, unlike the other animals, he's committed to none of them. Hence his immense biological superiority.

Socrates: I think I can follow that. But does he *feel* enlarged?

Schmidt: May I come in here to say that he does? Like Sir Hugo, I'm not clear about the biology of the matter, but I can tell you something about its psychology. A man comes to identify himself with his possessions, so that he isn't himself without them. He may be more vain of his façade than his face, and more hurt by the loss of a few tiles than many hairs. Growing up is growing outwards. Till a man feels so all-of-a-piece with the clothes he wears, and the horse he rides on, and the pen he writes with, that they no longer seem outside him, he has still to learn their use. The expert is one who, having incorporated his tools, is no longer aware of them – they've vanished into his physique. He doesn't sit on a seat in a boat that sails, *he* sails. He doesn't grasp a handle that holds a blade that cuts stone, *he* cuts stone. That's how he speaks and that's how he feels. Is it so long ago that you've forgotten, Socrates?

Socrates: By all the gods I do remember, now you remind me! And I was only an indifferent sculptor. Evidently you couldn't tell, by casual inspection, where Phidias stopped and his world began, for Phidias was no fixed quantity. I see quite clearly now that how big a man is depends on what he's up to – in both senses. This is very exciting!

Cowen: Well, unlike Dr. Schmidt, I'm concerned with objective facts and not subjective fancies. And I can assure you of this, Socrates: it isn't the mere 150 pounds of Homo Sapiens which has won him his place in the economy of nature. The organism that has survived and flourished and dominated the rest has done so by virtue of a much vaster and more elaborate physique – by what is, in fact, a new evolutionary departure.

Socrates: Aren't you forgetting it's artificial, Professor?

Cowen: To the impartial observer there's ultimately no such word, and the tool is as natural as the hand it completes.

Socrates: Then if you and I share the same house, my dear friend, we must share the same extended body. I suppose you'd call us a kind of Siamese twins! Ah, what a thought for a pair of lovers!

Cowen: Socrates! We aren't in ancient Greece!... I was about to say that, since your time, these extensions of man have multiplied and ramified in all directions, and become a huge network of roads and railways and wires and cables and pipes and what-not, all of which are held in common. Nowadays a man can drink at a mountain lake, and void his excrement into the sea, and live on the crops of another continent, and listen to music played on the other side of the world – all without setting foot outside his door. Instead of *going* to these places as an individual, he has contrived a way of *growing* up to them as a community. This is hard fact, though until recently it's not been quite respectable to mention it among scientists.

Socrates: Clearly the more you take in of a man's extended physique the less it is merely his, and the more it belongs to other men as well... So that's where he ceases and the outside world begins – where the human prolonged into the artificial at last meets nature.

Cowen: I'm afraid not. To cut off man from the rest of creatures is to do violence to the facts. The modern science of ecology has shown that species don't occur or survive or develop as things apart, but in great interlocking patterns of mutual dependence. The more you understand one organism the more you must have taken the others into account, so that to know one fully would be to know all. The bee doesn't make sense without the flower it pollinates, or the flower without the bee it provisions, any more than your muscle cells make sense without your brain cells and your liver cells. And now perhaps you'll see why I don't much like talking about living wholes – it's a problem to know where to stop. But if you insist on using the term, then it's to such broad vital patterns that you should apply it, rather than to the individuals or the species or the genera that have no meaning or existence apart from the patterns. In fact, I doubt whether anything short of the entire network of organisms, growing up as one living thing from the start, really merits the title of a living *whole*.

Canopus: My dear Cowen, look out! Mind what you say to Socrates. He called himself a babe in these things, but if ever there was an infant prodigy who needed watching it's this one! Believe me, he's not been wasting his time here: he's only to open his mouth to show he knows far more about us and our ideas than he admits to.

Socrates: Nobody can help picking up rumours here: it's a real gossip-shop. But a smattering of information isn't understanding, dear Sir Hugo; and it's understanding I so much lack... Don't let him put you off, Professor. I find your latest news most instructive.

Cowen: But it's bad news, Socrates, for your sky-monster. Or, if not, let's hear about its ecological links with other monsters billions of miles away, its sexual behaviour, its parentage and progeny, its diet and defecation, the nature of its protoplasm. You must see that any scientist who seriously began talking like this would pretty soon find himself in the hands of Dr. Schmidt here.

Socrates: Well, gentlemen, my consolation is that if I'm for the madhouse so are you, and I shall go on enjoying your delightful company. For my sky-monster, as you are pleased to call him, isn't mine but yours. As befits a pupil, I've contributed nothing positive to his description, or indeed to this whole discussion. All I claim to know is what you tell me. And what you've told me adds up to one thing...

Cowen: What on Earth's that?

Socrates: To *everything* on Earth, and inside her as well! To nothing less than a visible god – or let's say, our dear goddess – unveiled and evident, right under our noses. What we were straining after in the skies was here with us all the while. The ideal way of hiding this thing was to put it in full view!

Canopus: I was afraid something like this was coming!

Socrates: Well, it's come all right, whether you're afraid of it or not! Settling most of my remaining doubts, you've persuaded me that Earth herself is precisely one of your sky-monsters; and that – if anything – it's not *living* but *dead* heavenly bodies that call for proof.

Canopus: I'm glad to hear you had your doubts, Socrates. Are you quite sure you oughtn't still to have them?

Socrates: Let me explain what they were, and how you got rid of them – and then you shall judge for yourself.

When you granted that some of the heavenly bodies may, for all we know, be living creatures, the first thing that naturally occurred to me was to consider our own heavenly body the Earth – the only specimen that lies wide open to human inspection – just in case she should prove to be one of them. Certainly her build and behaviour agree wonderfully with the pattern you had laid down for a living sky-dweller. On the other hand, she is so unlike all the other creatures we know that to class her with them seemed absurd. And then I remembered your tale of levels of organization. The cell (you said) is a very different story from its molecules, and the many-celled animal a very different story from its cells. Equally, then, I should expect the living planet in its turn to be unique, and quite unpredictable from an examination of its animal and other parts. Planetary life, if it exists at all, is life of a new and supervenient order. And as it turned out, the surprising thing was not that this life should appear so unlike, but so like, the life of the order below. I noted, for instance, how Earth is not lacking in protoplasm – namely the protoplasm of all her creatures; how by her elaborate dance in the heavens (as you explained) she is always adjusting herself to her environment in a life-preserving manner; how she lives on the nourishment of sunlight; and how she has grown up to life of the most advanced kind from the merest rudiments – and you'd already drummed it into me that this life is her own natural growth and no invasion. As for her parentage, I gathered that she, with her fellow planets, had sprung from the Sun. Her offspring? Well, perhaps she is barren – not an unknown condition...

Canopus: Space-ships and artificial planetoids are on the way – make what you like of that, Socrates! But one thing you've forgotten – though Earth is beginning to spill Earthlets into the sky, she doesn't spill excrement.

Socrates: If the visible gods are a constipated crew, that's just as well, and most considerate of them. I shouldn't care to live in a celestial latrine! If Earth has a specially tidy way of dealing with her own waste, that's no more than might be expected of such an admirably self-contained creature. Actually, I should add, she does in fact spill excrement in the form of ammonia, marsh gas, and hydrogen, which are too volatile to be retained in the atmosphere… To sum up then, there proved to be nothing in my first objection: this living thing is no more different from the others we know than her order and scale and circumstances seem to call for. In any case I must follow your rule and take her as I find her, instead of trying to fit her into lesser moulds.

Canopus: But think of the bulk of her dead material, compared with the living part!

Socrates: That was my second objection. You'd already answered it. You had assured me that without such huge ballast she could never sail the skies and live. Besides, if we're forbidden to come to our observation of any living vessel with preconceived ideas, then we can't say in advance how such dead matter it can take on board without getting swamped. I remembered also your lesson – so hard to learn – that *all* the material of living things is inert in the last analysis, and that a good deal of it is inert anyhow. A man is not all cells, but also (as it were) the minimum of countryside in which they can get a livelihood. In a new and higher order of creature, then, the proportion of dead stuff to living might well be – might well *have* to be – very great indeed. And if there exist still higher orders, they are presumably still vaster, and incorporate a still greater proportion of stuff which, *considered by itself,* is stone dead.

Canopus: What I can't see is the connection between the so-called life of the planet and the life of its creatures.

Socrates: Neither could I. But by the time you gentlemen had finished with me I couldn't see anything else! Patiently you explained how, when you want to understand any vital

⁝

pattern, however insignificant, you're obliged to add and add to it till you've left out practically nothing terrestrial. Indeed you so overwhelmed me with evidence that I began to doubt, not Earth's life, but man's! If a man isn't all there, isn't a living *whole,* without the fabricated extensions he lives by, and the creatures he lives with, and the air and water and rock all ultimately live on, then where are his true boundaries? At the ends of the Earth. She is the full extent, the real and filled-out body of each of her creatures. For this is the lesson I've learned today: *only a heavenly body can live in heaven, and where else is there to live?*

Cowen: And you really learned all that from *us!*

Socrates: Largely from your self, Professor. Let me remind you of what you said about the emergence of new wholes. You explained (if you remember) that it's the specialization of the parts – their division of labour, so to say – which does the trick. And where will you find a completer or more subtle division of labour – mental as well as physical – than among the members of our Earth? If – judged by the degree of her organization and self-sufficiency – she is not an emergent whole, of a higher order than her parts, then I should like to know what in the universe is. A man? I very much doubt it! Or do *all* your rules go by the board when she's in question? What is it you've got against her?

Canopus: But why stop with the Earth, Socrates? If

you're going so far you've just got to go still further; and in any case, my dear fellow, you may as well be hanged for a sidereal sheep as a terrestrial lamb. You ought now to eat your words, and admit that the smallest complete and self-contained body that can live in the heavens isn't a planet after all, but a star – I mean, of course, one of those developed stars we call a solar system. The Earth can't do so, because without her Sun she's as dead as a man is without her. On your theory, the only true organisms are stars, and the rest mere organs. In fact I doubt whether even a solar system can be called complete and independent of the other stars, and of the Galaxy, and of the universe itself. This doesn't look too healthy for your gods: even they aren't all there.

Socrates: No doubt they'll take the blow with celestial fortitude! But is it so surprising to discover in the superhuman just such a system of subordination – just such a hierarchy of wholes and parts – as we found in the subhuman? Isn't this exactly what we need to fill the gap we found above man, and to balance the orders below him? Without it, isn't your universe as bottom-heavy as ours was top-heavy? I confess it's no great shock to me to find this ascending order of gods – planetary, sidereal, and perhaps even galactic, but all imperfect and finite – in which rank depends on the degree of completeness and independence achieved, and on the proportion of dead material raised to life. Something of the kind is exactly what you've prepared me for.

# NINE

Cowen: Then the sooner we prepare you to forget it the better!

Socrates: My dear Professor, I'm in your hands, and every bit as ready to unlearn as learn. Please go on, and if I've misunderstood you, just put me right.

Cowen: Living Earth, if you please! How *obviously* absurd!

Socrates: "The obvious is a polite name for the superficial. Beware first impressions, my friend: they never tell the whole story. It's the *scale* of the object that fools you. Magnify it, and the one is myriads of living things; diminish it, and they are one living thing." – Your very own words, Professor. Who's being fooled now – fooled by the *scale* of the planet?

Cowen: You don't understand. Let's get back to fundamentals. The real trouble, Socrates, is that you mistake the function of science. We aren't really interested in the kind of questions you've been asking, and which only invite, as we've seen, ridiculous answers. Observing is our job, not speculating. We try to examine phenomena with an unprejudiced eye and to describe them as clearly and economically as possible, preferably in mathematical terms; and we do so with a view to controlling them – or at least predicting them. And, let me tell you, this method certainly gets results. Till scholars stopped merely thinking about nature and man, and started really looking at them, science could never get under way, and one man's fancy was as good as another's. No wonder gods and angels flourished.

Socrates: You have my respectful congratulations, Professor! Observing man impartially, you've come to know him. Only let me share your knowledge, and I'll cheerfully stay for ever ignorant of the wide universe and all its gods, visible and invisible. What is man, body and soul? Only tell me that, and I'm your devoted disciple for eternity!

Cowen: When I can observe his soul I promise to start agitating myself about it. Observation of his body is quite enough to be getting on with.

Socrates: How do you go about it? Tell me in plain terms so that I can follow.

Cowen: Let me put the matter as simply as this – what a man's observed to be depends on where his observer is. At a certain distance, say ten feet, he sees the human body as a whole; a little closer, he sees some major part. And that's where observation usually began and ended until modern times. It was thought wicked to go much further into the matter. But the scientist isn't satisfied with the distant and superficial view of a man. He has instruments which bring him nearer, to places where he observes tissues, groups of cells, one cell in detail, and even its larger molecules. By such means, by close inspection, by going minutely into the thing, he finds out its real nature.

Socrates: I hope you can do all this without hurting the poor fellow too much.

Cowen: My dear Socrates, what do you take us for? We don't go round carving up perfectly healthy people just for the fun of exploring their insides. But when a man's ill it's often necessary to operate. That's to say, we drug or anaesthetize him and cut him open to deal with the diseased organ: and then, of course, we can learn a lot about him. And when he's dead we can dissect and analyse still further at our leisure.

Socrates: Let me get this quite clear, Professor. As you draw closer and closer to a man, you're presented with objects which though living are no longer human, and then objects which though material, are no longer living.

Canopus: Nor – if I may interrupt – is that the end. The physicist has ways and means of getting still closer, to where what you might call materiality vanishes.

Socrates: And a man amounts to all these aspects – all these regional appearances? He's what he's made out to be, not merely from one commonly accepted range or familiar viewpoint, but from as many as possible, no matter how odd his appearance may be? You're quite sure about that, Professor Cowen?

Cowen: Why yes.

Socrates: Very well then. Having taken the near view of him, let's go on to the far view. What, for instance, do you make of him at a distance of a mile.

Cowen: That's easy. I make nothing of him. At that distance he's vanished. Other things appear.

Socrates: But didn't something of the kind happen when you approached him? In that case I can't see the force of your objection, Professor, and must ask you to go on and tell me what you find when you recede from him.

Cowen: Is that an order? Well, I guess I've let myself in for it! If I move away from the man, and he happens to be sitting at home, I see first a house, and then a district, and then a city, and then bigger and bigger pieces of the map (so to speak), and then...

Socrates: Yes? Out with it!

Cowen: Why the Earth, of course, and then the Sun, and eventually the Galaxy. And much comfort may that bring you Socrates! We were talking about a *man*. Trust you to drag in your priceless celestial monsters, which are something quite different.

Socrates: Which of his many appearances would you say is more different from a man, his particles or his planet? If the first is all right, why not the second? But let me remind you we don't yet know what a man is. That's the very matter at issue, and we mayn't prejudge it by saying in advance he can't – and by heavens he shan't – be this or that, or by picking and choosing amongst his aspects as the fancy takes us. We can only (it's you I'm quoting) look and see with an unprejudiced eye, from as many viewpoints as possible, and humbly take what we find. And what we find includes (you assure me) not only non-living particles and living cells and what is called a human body, but a home, a city, a country, a planet, and a star, in that order. All of which agrees very well with what you've already said: namely, that a man is incomplete, not all there, without his greater or extended body, which includes a home, a city, a country, a planet, and a star – all much as before... Yes, Archdeacon?

Brown: As a mere layman, the distant view seems to me to include far too much that isn't man.

Socrates: And as another mere layman, the near view seems to me to *exclude* far too much that *is* man. Which is worse? But again, both objections are ruled out because they beg the question: what is man?

Brown: In spite of what Cowen has said, I feel sure that science plumps for the near view of man.

Cowen: There's at least one good reason for that: the near view of man is much more useful to him than the far view.

Socrates: I suggest we discuss the question *what is useful?* some other time, and for the present stick to the question *what is man?* And if (breaking your own rule of impartiality) you insist on preferring one view of him to another, haven't you already preferred the far view? If the near view means drugging and wounding and killing your subject, and then dissolving the corpse in the acid bath of your physics, isn't it largely the product of your own violence, and to that extent unrealistic? It means the destruction by degrees of everything you're examining – the human, the vital, even the material. I don't doubt it is necessary and immensely useful and altogether admirable in its way, but it is the very opposite of the stern realism you profess. For realism you must take the far view, the one which (I quote you again) makes sense of what you're examining, instead of nonsense and in the end nothing. It progressively heals your victim, putting back the missing parts, reversing his decomposition, bringing him more and more to life, restoring independence and individuality. And we've found it leads us, by easy stages, to the Earth and Sun which complete him and all men, and without which he is neither human nor alive nor material. In a word, it takes us to heaven... And so, my dear Professor, your foolproof method of unprejudiced observation, which was going to be the death of the gods, looks like granting them a new lease of life. Do you still stand by the method?

Cowen: Of course I do, provided it's properly used. In this case it isn't. Let me tell you one little thing you've conveniently overlooked. When the observer moves away from a man, the direction of his gaze is almost sure to alter as each new object comes into view. It shifts (for instance) from the upper part of the body to the middle, from some outlying part of the house to the building as a whole, from the building to the town's centre, from the town to the centre or capital of the country, from the country to the Earth's centre, from the Earth's to the Sun's... But in that case the observer's cheating. He's letting his eye wander.

Socrates: Didn't much the same thing happen when you were approaching your man instead of receding?

Cowen: Well...

Brown: Excuse me, Professor Cowen. Surely the trouble is you're both ignoring the subject himself. Instead of quarrelling over his body – dead or alive – why not ask him how it feels to be a man? You might find his answer helpful.

Socrates: All right, Archdeacon. Let's ask him about this centre-shifting the Professor's so concerned about. Doesn't he reply that, from his side, he's always having a similar experience – for instance, when for the time being he transfers his loyalty from his solitary self to his home and family, and from his family to his town, and from his town to his country, and so on? Isn't this correction of his initial off-centredness the precise counterpart of his observer's similar correction? Don't the inner and the outer story of your man admirably support each other here?

No, my dear Professor, it is the observer with the *fixed* stare who cheats, and this latest objection of yours only turns out to be a further confirmation of our picture of man in the universe.

# TEN

Cowen: If only your common sense, Socrates, weren't inversely proportional to your ingenuity! A man's got a pretty good working knowledge of what he is and what he isn't. Try hitting out in his direction and you'll soon share his knowledge! Or just ask him.

Socrates: What's common sense? If you mean the consensus of opinion through the ages, and not merely in the 20th century, I think you'll find it on the whole favourable to our conclusions. But that's by the way. I'm afraid, my dear Professor, you're craftily shifting your ground, and consulting your man instead of observing him. Well, if you insist on bringing in his soul – which just now you insisted on leaving out – I'm the last one to make a fuss.

Cowen: Soul? I've no use for the word. But I'll go so far as to admit that a man has two aspects – call them, instead of his body and soul, his observer's view in and his own view out. Or, if you prefer, others' experience of him and his experience of others. The first (which you call his body) was an unknown quantity till it was taken over by physical science with its strictly empirical methods; the second (which you call his mind) will remain even more vague and chaotic till it's taken over by a psychological science with equally empirical methods. This isn't my line

– and I doubt whether Dr. Schmidt here will agree with me – but if I were going to tackle the view out I should treat it as far as possible like the view in. I should deal only with its concrete sense contents – I mean the sort of thing that has colour and shape and motion. Then I should have a chance of getting somewhere. Certainly I shouldn't look for a ghost called a Soul, or for those ghosts of a ghost called functions or faculties of a soul – mysterious sprites which you can neither pin down nor prevent from multiplying *ad infinitum*. What psychology needs is rigid birth-control amongst its ideas.

Schmidt: I doubt whether it will go to Professor Cowen's establishment for the apparatus!

Socrates: Why not try taking the Professor's proposal seriously, Dr. Schmidt? Let's not talk of the soul but of experience, and not of experience as some mysterious entity or bundle of will-o'-the-wisp functions, but of its shaped and moving contents. What are they? But I don't need to ask: you've already told me. Your experience is of such things as molecules, cells, organs, many-celled creatures, homes, towns, stretches of country, planets, stars, galaxies. In short, your 'mind' (or view-out-from-you) is just as variable as your 'body' (or view-in-to-you). It seems, even, as if they come to much the same thing. Though with this difference: the view-in is of one particular organ or man or house or planet or star – namely *this* one, while the view-out is of the *others*. That's to say, the inside and the outside accounts of a man are pretty well matched, each confirming and supplementing the other. Whichever way, then, you take a man – whether you look with him or at him – you are apt to find heavenly bodies, animal bodies, material bodies. You gentlemen are my authority.

Cowen: Whatever a man may look at and look like, at any rate he never *felt* like a bloated planet!

Socrates: Forgive me for mentioning it, my dear Professor, but you seem to be shifting your ground once more. It looks as if, instead of confining yourself to clear sense contents, you're smuggling in one of your abhorred mental faculties or functions. But again, who cares? Believe me when I say I'm not trying to catch you out, but simply to get at what you really mean. I think your knowledge so precious that I don't mind how I coax or screw it out of you. But let's get on. Having first considered what a man looks like to others, and then what they look like to him, let's turn – as you suggest – to what he feels like, and see whether that can help us. I imagine this is the point where you come in, Dr. Schmidt.

Schmidt: Well, of course, the trouble is that even if you know what you feel you often can't find words for it; and even if you can they probably don't mean the same to you as to me. What's needed for these interchanges is a stable and generally accepted verbal currency.

Socrates: I see the difficulty. What about taking as an experiment some of our small change, and seeing whether it keeps its value? Consider, for instance, the little word *here*. You have the feeling that something is *here*, Dr. Schmidt, and other things are not. All right then. When you tell your doctor you have a pain *here*, where do you mean?

Schmidt: In this part of my body and not that.

Socrates: And when you ask your child to come *here*?

Schmidt: I wish him to come to this part of the room.

Socrates: And when you invite a party of friends *here*?

Schmidt: I'm asking them to my house.

Socrates: Now supposing you were told that some foreigners had arrived *here*?

Schmidt: I should take it they'd arrived in my country.

Socrates: And when people talk of Martians landing *here* one day?

Schmidt: They mean on Earth, of course.

Socrates: Well, there's unstable currency for you! There's inflation! What you feel to be *here* may vary from your aching belly to your star. And, along with it, what you feel to be *there* varies from all the other members of your body to all the other stars. Now supposing we tried out, instead of *here* and *there*, such pairs of words as *this* and *that*, *now* and *then*, *small* and *big*, *fast* and *slow*, *near* and *far*, *mine* and *theirs* – do you think we should find exactly the same kind of swelling and shrinking?

Schmidt: Certainly.

Socrates: Would you agree that we can neither do without these words nor cure their elasticity, but only try to understand it and use it intelligently? And that this elasticity in our language, so far from being a monstrous defect, is in fact required for putting over the elasticity we feel, that is very much a part of our nature?

Schmidt: I can't deny it.

Socrates: Who could? A creature who in the same breath can say "my planet and my country and my stomach" or "this millennium and this year and this half second", and who can off-handedly talk about *near* galaxies yet *distant* neighbours, and *tiny* stars yet *huge* stones – such a creature is either no fixed quantity or else a gigantic fraud. Let's take him at his word. He talks as he feels. And this elasticity of his inner feeling agrees perfectly with the elasticity of his outer appearance to others, and of their outer appearance to him. In other words, Professor, it turns out that whether we take what a man looks like, or what others look like to him, or what he feels like, we find much the same stages of growth and shrinking.

Cowen: I distrust these verbal conjuring tricks.

Socrates: Very well, then, let's try another kind of evidence. Dr. Schmidt, does your clinical experience contradict or bear out what we've been saying?

Schmidt: Well, Socrates, I'm bound to admit that I've known a patient identify himself with one part of his body and treat the rest as alien and even hostile. And everyone knows a man may, for longer or shorter periods, so identify himself with his family or his possessions, or with his city or his country, or even (if it comes to interplanetary war) with his planet, that he feels hurt when they are hurt, and makes their fortune his fortune, and lives and dies for them in utter contempt for his welfare as a private individual. To tell the truth, anyone who lacked all such feelings would be out of his mind.

Socrates: Now tell us: is this expansion and contraction – so strongly felt and acted upon – illusory?

Schmidt: Not at all. In fact the word illusory, used like that, is surely meaningless.

Canopus: I say, Schmidt, aren't you treading on dangerous ground? Once you start blurring the lines that divide one mind from another, you can say goodbye to personal responsibility. I wouldn't answer for the moral consequences.

Socrates: Do you mind, Sir Hugo, if we go on asking what's true, and put off asking what's expedient till another time? As you may have heard, I've not been in the habit of playing for safety in my search for truth, and I really don't feel like starting at this late stage – hemlock or no hemlock!

Brown: May I interrupt? I think Sir Hugo, in his proper anxiety to keep the distinction between selves, is overlooking something. We live by continually making and breaking that distinction. This is the way I see it: each man has two selves – a lesser which excludes other selves, and a greater which includes them; and without the conflict-in-unity of these two he is neither moral, nor rational, nor even human. To my lesser self, a big star's a bright one, an important town's a convenient one, a good man's an obliging one – everything's judged subjectively, by its effects on me alone. My greater self, on the other hand, looks at things objectively, from the point of view of all the selves it embraces. My lesser self feels for and takes responsibility for itself only, but my greater self feels for and takes responsibility for many others. In fact the really good man cuts himself off from nobody and nothing, and takes upon his shoulders the burden of the whole world. It's the devil who, by insisting always on his separate and unique self, his inviolable personality, loses it. Paradoxically, you can achieve real distinctness and distinction only by achieving their opposites also.

Socrates: Inspired words, Archdeacon, but alas a little over my head! Shall we now get back to the evidence of science? Dr. Schmidt, have you found anything to warrant our speaking of men's minds or souls as quite separate from one another, and only able to communicate indirectly through the sense and bodily expression?

Schmidt: I'm bound to say I haven't, Socrates. I can't even imagine what kind of evidence could possibly justify such talk.

Socrates: On the other hand, do you know of any evidence which supports the opposite view, and suggests hidden connections between minds, or an underlying unity?

Schmidt: Indeed I do. Though Sir Hugo may not agree, I think anyone who fairly examines the case for clairvoyance and telepathy must own they've been proved over and over again. And I don't see, after that, how we can go on talking of the individual psyche as if it were encased in toughened armour-plate.

Socrates: Though no doubt you doctors have in practice to treat your patients as quite separate entities?

Canopus: Each getting his own bill, you may be sure!

Schmidt: Some of us are interested in collective behaviour, and we can't very well avoid using such terms as the mentality of races, national feeling, crowd hysteria, mass neurosis. Others go in for group psychiatry, the curative effects of which actually depend on building up what we can only call a group mind, or something of the sort. Again, it's often impossible to disentangle a mother's psyche from her child's. In short – to use a spatial metaphor – we find many degrees of fusion or temporary overlapping among minds.

Canopus: Isn't this overlapping exceptional?

Schmidt: On the contrary, Sir Hugo, it's the *distinct* psyche – the truly differentiated personality – which is exceptional. It takes years of careful education and mental discipline to detach ourselves in any marked degree from the mass mind, and most of us never manage it.

Socrates: Then there does exist a super-individual mentality of some kind?

Schmidt: The evidence, my dear Socrates, forces many of us towards just that, obliging us to postulate an Unconscious which is the origin and common ground of every psyche. If we want to understand a man's mentality, we can't – as I've already pointed out – separate it from the mentality of his ancestors, who go right back to the primitive human and even animal stock. It seems as if the great genealogical tree, in which all that have lived on Earth are physically continuous, has also a psychological aspect. If we knew how, I believe we could dig out, beneath the surface of every individual mind, layer upon layer of collective mind, each older and more comprehensive than the last, till we got down to the common foundation and source of all. Nor is this mere theory: in practice we find that repressing the contents of these deeper layers of the mind can lead to mental illness and even madness.

Socrates: There's a rumour going around here that this Unconscious of yours is a very unpleasant piece of work, vastly inferior to the conscious mind, and amoral if not immoral – a merely animal mentality, in fact.

Schmidt: True enough, it often presents such an aspect. But to many of its students it shows also a very different face – a wisdom and purpose that are quite remarkable. Indeed its most important function is seemingly to correct all the while the dangerous one-sidedness of our conscious minds, making good what we lack and so restoring us to wholeness and health. We resist its warnings at our peril. And the seer and the artist – the innovator of any kind – is nothing if not its vehicle.

Socrates: And if that isn't a composite portrait of the gods I'm not Socrates, and certainly not the Socrates who was guided – is guided at this very moment – by divine promptings! After this, my dear Dr. Schmidt, you really can't tell me you don't believe in divinities – surname them the Unconscious if you must!… But now what I should so much like to hear is something about the thoughts that run through this wonderful Mind – it's contents, if you must put it that way.

Schmidt: That would take us all night.

Socrates: Won't you treat us to one or two samples?

Schmidt: Well, I suppose I'll have to let the cat out of the bag, and risk getting into trouble with my friends here.

Mother Earth and the Sun – the Sun which seems to stand for the wholeness of man – figure largely and often in the Collective Unconscious, or so some of us find. And no doubt that's why, my dear Socrates, you're so much under their influence. Your visible gods are very much at home in those deeper levels of your mind which you share with others, and it's quite natural they should pop up their heads from time to time.

Socrates: Then my ostensibly private idea of the living Earth really stems from the common mind of all the living, which again stems from Earth herself, so that in me – and others like me – our dear goddess comes to self-awareness. For if there's one thing we've settled it's that her creatures aren't parasites she's somehow picked up, or visitors who've somehow dropped in: body and mind arise from her and are completed in her. It is she who lies at the foot of this ancestral tree which is at once physical and psychical: indeed she is the nourishing root itself. You've indicated that every mind you study is not only continuous with her mind, which appears godlike in wisdom and healing power, but has access to the whole of it – in principle at least. No wonder she herself figures among its ideas.

To sum up, then, it appears there are ways – and doubtless many ways – in which a man, by ceasing to cut himself off from his fellow men and fellow creatures, may find that he shares the life of the gods, yet without ceasing to be a man. The realization of himself is the realization of a far greater self than is first apparent.

Brown: And tradition is certainly with you there, Socrates. It has been the more or less universal intuition of mankind that man isn't only man, but is capable of conscious union with that which transcends him.

# ELEVEN

Schmidt: I must warn you, Socrates, that my business is the psychological world, and when you start matching it up with the physical world I wash my hands of you. Of course you're free to look round for graded bodes to weight down the graded Unconscious; and so far as you are psychologically driven to do this I'm professionally interested – couldn't be more so. But whether the results are objectively valid is quite another question.

Brown: Really, Dr. Schmidt, we can't let you get away with it as easily as that! It was you and not Socrates who talked about the ancestral tree of life as at once physical and psychical, and we're all agreed that Earth is the root of that tree.

Socrates: And every branch and twig too, Archdeacon. Besides, I remember another warning I've had today – that bodiless minds are suspect, to say the least. I see you believe in them after all, Dr. Schmidt. No? Well then, we have on our hands these three items – a general distrust of bodiless minds, plus an Earth-mind lacking a body, plus an Earth-body lacking a mind. Add the three and what's the answer?

Schmidt: Well, whatever it is, Socrates, it lies outside the sphere of the psychologist as such.

Socrates: Are you sure? When you talk like that, Dr. Schmidt, I can't help wondering whether you're not neglecting your own business. Surely the essential thing about the gods is their tremendous actuality. If they can never be more real to you than shadowy symbols or dream figures – if they're incapable of taking you by storm and bowling you over completely – then they aren't gods at all but poor washed-out figments. You say the Sun is the *symbol* of your wholeness, but isn't that because he's also – as indeed we've seen – its *reality?* And what becomes of that reality without him, the great Helios? I imagine no man ever basked in the rays of a solar symbol, or found it good for the crops; and if the symbol moved him it was because, behind it, shone the terrific being the symbol stood for. Doesn't your refusal (in the face of all your own evidence and arguments) to admit the *objective* existence of the gods – your reduction of them to merely psychic elements – amount to their almost complete repression? And repression, you tell me, is so bad for you! Is your Unconscious perfectly satisfied with such miserable wraiths of the glorious gods of heaven, and likely to give you no further trouble on their account? Are you certain your resistance to them – flying in the face of reason, as it seems to me – isn't itself a sign of mental trouble? On this subject, are you moderns quite sane?... Forgive me! Here I am, rashly trespassing far into your sacred professional precincts, and no doubt making a perfect fool of myself!

Schmidt: Not at all, my dear Socrates: get it off your chest! It'll do you good. If you were my patient, I'd point out that it's quite normal, at some stage in the treatment, for you to launch an attack on the analyst; in fact it may be part of the cure. As it is, I'm not arguing with you, and certainly not contradicting you. You can count on my warm sympathy and understanding. I know that all you say about the burning reality of the gods is immensely true and important for you.

Socrates: In my day *true* meant true *for everyone.* Has the word ceased to have any meaning for you people? Or is it only psychologists who are allowed to make it mean what they like? Of all the men I've met in this place, Doctor, I find you the most baffling. It's not merely as though we spoke quite different languages, but as though we hailed from quite different worlds. Surely you are one of the gods in mortal guise – a god who can afford to look down on rational creatures with benevolent pity, because he's gifted with a wisdom so divine that it transcends even reason!

# TWELVE

Cowen: You see what you've let us in for, Schmidt! This Unconscious of yours may be all very well for the consulting room, but it oughtn't to be let loose outside – especially when Socrates is around. For God's sake let's get back on to solid ground again, and instead of making Socrates free gifts of more and more dream material, do something to wake him up.

Socrates: Ah, Professor, if only you would be so kind! For twenty-three centuries – on and off – I've been trying to rouse myself from this intellectual stupor of mine, and now at last...

Cowen: That'll do, Socrates. I'm getting rather tired of this parade of humility; we saw through your act long ago, and know just how much you think of yourself. But now – to get back to business – here's a straight question I'd like to put to you, and no crooked answers please. If Earth is a living creature, let's hear something about her anatomy. I think it was Leonardo, of all people, who talked about rocks as her bones, rivers as her blood, trees and plants as her hair. What drivel! But can you do any better?

Socrates: I can do nothing but rely on you gentlemen. And one thing you've taught me is to look at the object as it's given at each level of observation, and not confuse it with what was given at other levels of observation. As you retire from the planet, what do you find? Well, you've mentioned a wonderful network that encompasses her. It's for you to tell *me* how it would look.

Cowen: Nothing doing! This mouse is beginning to recognize a Socratic trap – well baited with cajolery – when it sees one!

Brown: Come, play fair, Professor... Very well then, I'll try to help you, Socrates. The planet is covered – in some places thickly and in others very thinly – with this great net of roads and the buildings that line them, railways, pipelines, cables, sewers, canals, telegraphs, and so on, and at the intersections are knots of various sizes which are cities and towns and villages. You'd be able to see a great deal of this pattern as you traveled away from the Earth.

Socrates: Does it show any sign of life?

Brown: Well, you'd see the knots glowing in the dark, and if you looked long enough you'd see it sending out new feelers (so to speak) all the time, and growing here and dying off there. You might just make out the flow of its traffic, and note that it's more abundant by day than by night. In fact, there would be material for a lifetime's study.

Socrates: Does this object have anything to say for itself?

Brown: Well, that's a queer way of putting it, but if you were suitably fixed up with a radio receiver you'd certainly find it both talkative and musical.

Cowen: Isn't it time someone informed Socrates that

this network is neither a living thing nor the organ of a greater one, but simply a lot of men you're too far off to see, plus their dead works?

Socrates: Just as a man isn't a man at all, but simply a lot of cells you're too far off to see, plus *their* dead works! No, Professor, I've learned my lesson too well to fall for that one! What's the sense of my taking up this distant observation post if I won't accept what I find there, just as it's given? I've forgotten about men when I'm examining their Earth – forgotten about them as completely as you've done when you're examining their particles. Following your example, I'm looking, not arguing. In fact, I don't know what on Earth you're talking about: all I can see from here is this fine network shining at night, sending out feelers, growing and decaying. And if for a moment I were to doubt its life I can always try listening to it... Well, Professor, if you're on the lookout for genuine planetary organs, here's a whole set for you to be getting on with.

Cowen: All very specious, and quite unsound. You're using the word organ in a very odd sense.

Socrates: I'm observing a very odd creature. If you find Earth's anatomy peculiar, why that's only to be expected; have you forgotten already that when you and Sir Hugo were constructing your celestial monster you ruled out almost all limbs and organs like ours as quite unsuitable for life in the sky? Except, I think, eyes. This creature could do with gigantic eyes, you said, capable of seeing much further into the heavens than we can. Well now, Sir Hugo, has she any?

Canopus: You know perfectly well she has – of a sort. Our great observatories – *there* are eyes for you, and on a planetary scale too, weighing thousands of tons, with a huge range, and revealing countless stars you never saw. But I'm afraid, Socrates, they aren't enormous balls of jelly growing out of the face of the Earth and equipped with lids and lashes and tear-glands. I happen to know, because I helped to design and build and man one of the things! If they are Earth's eyes, they're her glass eyes – artificial to a degree.

Socrates: But evidently far from sightless. If they're so wonderfully efficient, their glass is nothing for her to feel ashamed of. Nor is their artificiality. Rather the reverse: what other creature can take the credit for its own eyes? In any case, the Professor has assured us that *artificial* is an adjective that doesn't appear in the impartial observer's dictionary; very likely the human eye would appear to its cells to be as artificial as your observatory does to you, if ever they got around to thinking about it. Besides, just as the human eye is nothing without its cellular members, so this Earth eye is nothing without its human members – without Sir Hugo and his distinguished colleagues; and they're natural enough, I think. Here, then, are the eyes that not only enable this heavenly body to see its companions clearly, but are actually developed with that very purpose clearly in mind. Well, Professor Cowen, are we doing any better than your friend Leonardo da Vinci?

Cowen: I doubt it. These planetary eyes, as you're pleased to call them, aren't eyes at all in my sense of the term. They have nothing in common with the animal eye, and work on quite different principles.

Socrates: Which, if true, is not surprising. But let's get the facts from Sir Hugo. I'd like to ask him, for instance, how he would judge the distance of the Moon.

Canopus: I'm afraid Professor Cowen isn't going to like my answer much. Your own eyes, Socrates, are some three inches apart, with the result that each gets a slightly different view of me, and this helps you to place me. Similarly two observatories, say four thousand miles apart on the face of the Earth, get slightly different views of the Moon, and this helps us to place her.

Socrates: So a heavenly body, like an earthly one, needs at least a pair of eyes in its head if it's not to live in a flat world.

Cowen: That's all very fine when you're talking about the Earth, a mere planet. But what about your star-gods – the Sun for instance? Are there observatories on his vast surface, spaced so far apart that he, in turn, can get a binocular view of his fellow stars, and so read off their distances? I always thought the Sun was uncomfortably warm for that sort of thing. How would you like the appointment of solar Astronomer Royal, Sir Hugo?

Canopus: Well, here's another little surprise for you, my dear Professor. I've held the appointment – and liked it! Let me explain. You seem to have forgotten that the Sun we're talking about isn't merely the hot central mass, but also the system of its planets: it is the developed or expanded star, which includes the Earth and her orbit. Now when we note the direction of one of the nearer stars in March (let's say) and then again in September, we find it has slightly altered, because our two observation points are on opposite sides of our orbit and 186 million miles apart – a truly solar dimension. This difference of direction enables us to judge the star's distance.

Socrates: I take it that the same observatories which serve as planetary 'eyes' when placing the planets, serve as solar 'eyes' when placing the stars?

Canopus: That's about it.

Socrates: To sum up, then: it takes a man whose eyes are a few inches apart to place another man, a planet whose 'eyes' are thousands of miles apart to place another planet, and a star whose 'eyes' are millions of miles apart to place another star. At each level the observer and his sensory equipment match the observed. Am I right, Sir Hugo?

Canopus: You put it quaintly.

Socrates: Well, Professor Cowen, we seem to be making headway in our search for organs that befit a heavenly body... Now a little while back, Sir Hugo, you said that if a heavenly body is to be as well adapted to its environment as we are to ours, it will be alive to influences we never feel; in which case it will need special sensory equipment to register them. Do you know of anything like that?

Canopus: I do indeed; though again, Socrates, you and I don't use the same language. We've a great variety of instruments for detecting and measuring the radiation that arrives from outer space. We've devices for analyzing the light that comes to us from the stars, so that we can tell what they are made of. We even have means of 'listening', so to speak, to stars we can't see.

Socrates: And don't forget, Professor Cowen, that all this sensory equipment, along with the mind it serves grows as naturally from our heavenly body as leaves from a tree – according to you. It didn't drop out of the skies.

# THIRTEEN

Cowen: What sort of nonsense is this? All this talk of planetary awareness cuts no ice at all. A planet is as a planet does. And what it does altogether fails to impress me. You argue that it knows what it's up to, but I beg leave to judge it by its behaviour, which is utterly monotonous and lacking any sign of life. Sense organs and mind which make no difference to action are suspect – to put it as mildly as possible.

Socrates: I don't quite follow you, Professor. We've established that Earth's motions are admirably life-preserving, and that she's well aware of the fact. Now if wandering is suicide – and in this case I'm told it is – then failing to wander is no sign of stupidity. You don't call a man a silly ass for neither rushing straight into his fireplace nor rushing miles away from it: he shows his good sense by sitting down quietly and enjoying the warmth at the proper distance. If, then, the planet's orderly habits are any indication at all, they certainly don't argue against her intelligence: rather the reverse. No, my dear Professor, you'll have to think up a better one that that!

Cowen: She doesn't *will* her behaviour. Even if it's life-preserving and known to be so, it isn't intentional. It just happens.

Socrates: But my dear fellow, it was only a few minutes ago that you ruled out the *will*, and all faculties or functions of that sort – ghosts of a ghost is what you called them... Well, never mind. Let's treat your new objection seriously. What do we mean, Dr. Schmidt, when we talk of a man acting intentionally?

Schmidt: I don't know about others, but when I say a man does something *automatically* I mean he does it without thinking. When I say he does it intentionally I mean, firstly, that he thinks about it, and at least considers the possibility of doing something else instead; and secondly, that he isn't actually pushed into doing it from outside. If this doesn't satisfy you, and you start talking about 'free will', then you're in danger of plunging headfirst into a bottomless pit of metaphysics – which I'm staying out of.

Socrates: Thank you. Now Sir Hugo, you've told us that the Earth, through her astronomers, knows exactly how she moves in heaven. Can you now tell us how, through them, she works out her path?

Canopus: That's rather a tall order, Socrates. What I can do is tell you how they went about the job till recently. To determine her orbit, the astronomers supposed that the Earth is subject to two laws – the law of inertia and the law of gravity. The first refers to her tendency to go on in a straight line, which means flying off at a tangent; the second refers to her tendency to fall straight into the Sun. Now the interesting thing is that his calculations didn't give her credit for obeying both these laws at once. On the contrary, he assumed she disobeys first the one and then the other, so that her path is shaped like a ratchet; but the cogs of this ratchet are so small that her path is smoothed out into the compromise of a curve, which obeys both laws alike.

Socrates: In other words, some hesitation or indecision is the price of her awareness, and her full consciousness of her lawful behaviour involves at least token defiance of the law. Her reckoning means she knows what she's doing, and the steps of her reckoning mean that she thinks of doing otherwise. So much for the first of Dr. Schmidt's criteria. Now for the second. Sir Hugo, is there any exterior force which pushes the Earth round her orbit?

Canopus: We gave up that idea many years ago.

Socrates: Then the Earth complies with our conditions of freedom, and no more deserves to be called an automaton than you do, my dear Professor. In fact, the boot's surely on the other foot. I very much question whether you, or any of us men – as men – are half as conscious of our acts as she is of hers, or as deliberate, or as free from outside interference. It is we lesser beings who so often behave unintentionally, as if in a dream. It is we who are always making silly mistakes and getting pushed around. She, our dear goddess, is far above these things! The stick you were going to beat her with, Professor, has come down on your own head!

Cowen: If you think it's knocked me out, Socrates, you're very much mistaken. Look out for yourself! As Canopus implied, this ratchet of his is pretty well worn out: having served its purpose in the history of science, it's now for the scrap-heap.

Socrates: Can it be that the planet is in danger, then, of losing her freedom, and becoming a creature of mere habit? That is an alarming possibility which we must examine as soon as possible. Meanwhile, it is enough for the argument that she has, at any rate in the recent past, enjoyed the freedom – the dithering, if you like – which Sir Hugo has described.

Cowen: What you've been saying is all very plausible so long as you cunningly ignore this planet's remote past, before the days of astronomy, before life itself arrived. She moved then very much as she does now, yet without any trace of mind.

Socrates: There's the behaviour and there's the intention; only the snag is they don't always come at the same time. We find temporal displacement, so to say. Is that what you mean?

Cowen: Precisely. And it's a snag which is quite fatal for your darling goddess, Socrates.

Socrates: Dear me, this certainly looks serious! But before going into mourning for her, let's take a look at our own condition. Let's make sure there's no similar displacement in man himself. Does he ever intend first and act afterwards, Professor?

Cowen: A superfluous question – of course he does.

Socrates: And, conversely, does he ever act first and intend afterwards? Have you never, when suddenly tripping up, put out your hand – quicker than thought – to save yourself, and meant what you did after you'd done it?

Cowen: Well...

Socrates: Again, as a foetus in the womb and a baby in the cradle, didn't you grow and act in every respect so as to make for the man Waldo Cowen with all his fine purposes, yet without the hint of a purpose at the time? Yet you don't *seem* Professor, to regard yourself as an automaton or a talking doll; and if in fact you do, you can hardly expect us to take your argument seriously. How can the man who intends his present life and its future continuance fail to intend also *all* that made it what it is – even to the whole of Earth's history – no matter how unintentional it was when it happened? Aren't intention and responsibility in creatures *always* rather late developments; and when they come, can they ever disclaim their roots?

Cowen: Well...

Socrates: I didn't catch what you said.

Cowen: Oh all right. I withdraw that particular objection.

Socrates: I think you'd better. There aren't many rude names you can call our goddess without calling yourself them too. In any case, why not go by what she says? Has she never – using the only mouths she's blessed with – admitted any responsibility for her behaviour? Is there no history of anxiety about the continuance of these cosmic processes?

Brown: You know very well there is, Socrates. Millions have claimed that, without the constant help of their religious rites, nature would fail and the heavens come to a standstill. They felt responsible for Earth and Sun, and took their responsibility very seriously.

Socrates: And with what knife, my dear Professor, do you propose to sever this feeling from the heavenly bodies which – as you insist – naturally produce it?

# FOURTEEN

**B**rown: There's just one thing that's worrying me, Socrates. Your gods have so many mouths, and the mouths say so many things. How, for instance, can astronomers differ as much as they do about the planets, if their thinking is really the Earth's; and about the stars, if their thinking is really the Sun's?

Socrates: Tell us, Sir Hugo, is there in fact much clash of opinion on these subjects? How far do you astronomers agree about the composition, distances, sizes, and motions of the planets and stars?

Canopus: I'm happy to say that the area of agreement is very large indeed compared with the area of differences. In fact it's one of the chief secrets of modern progress in astronomy that there exists a vast and growing body of accepted knowledge, and only at the expanding fringes is there much room for conflicting views. How unlike psychology, for example! They tell me there are as many schools of thought as eminent psychologists – is there one of them who'd agree with everything Schmidt's said here tonight? But astronomy unites the Earth, as one of its most famous practitioners used to say.

Socrates: And no wonder, if it's her own accomplishment... And now, Dr. Schmidt, please tell us about man. Does he ever hold at one time conflicting views about other men? Is his mind ever divided against itself?

Schmidt: The condition isn't merely known: it's normal. None of us is consistent. And in some cases of mental illness a man's personality may split into two or more quite contradictory phases; so that, for instance, his hand may record memories while his lips are denying all knowledge of them.

Socrates: There's your answer, Archdeacon. Apparently this planet and star are in quite good mental shape, and stand in no need of treatment from Dr. Schmidt. They suffer no more from doubts and hesitation than is good for them, and could teach us men a thing or two.

Brown: So far, I'm with you. But I'm still very puzzled, Socrates. When one astronomer looks at another, it's a mere man who's looking; but let him turn to Mars, and – wonderful transformation! – it's the whole Earth who's looking. I find it difficult enough to imagine how, by the mere act of glancing at the red planet, he's united with any other men who happen to be doing the same thing; but how he's united also with all the other men who are *not* looking at Mars, and all the other animals and plants, and all the rocks and seas of Earth, is quite beyond my comprehension. It sounds very odd to me.

Cowen: Odd is right! Impossible, I'd say. The astronomer's experience – I don't care if he's contemplating Mars or another astronomer or a pinhead – belongs to only *one* observer, and he's a man, neither more nor less.

Socrates: Perhaps you'd enlarge on that a bit, Professor, and explain what actually happens when, for example, one man sees another.

Cowen: Do we have to go into all that? It's a long and involved story.

Socrates: The briefest summary will do.

Cowen: Well, if you insist. What happens is roughly this. Light from the object reaches the observer's eye, passes through the lens, and forms a little picture on the screen at the back. This screen is made up of a special kind of cells and a substance called the visual purple. The light causes chemical changes in the visual purple, and the cells are disturbed by the changes.

Socrates: So it's these cells which actually get an impression of the object?

Cowen: Not by a long way. They pass on the disturbance to other cells – communicating ones – which pass it on to still other cells in a certain region of the brain. And it's not until this terminus is reached that the object is seen.

Socrates: But my dear Professor, that can't be the end of the story. You haven't mentioned the man's feet yet, or his hands, or his bones, or his stomach, or his ears and nose and tongue!

Cowen: Of course I haven't. They aren't involved.

Socrates: But a moment ago you said it's nothing less

than a *man* that sees. Now you're leaving out almost all of him. Again, you said there's only *one* observer. Now you seem to be talking of myriads.

Cowen: I admit the two stories sound hopelessly incompatible, but in practice they aren't at all. Why they aren't I don't know. We just have to accept the paradox: the whole man sees, yet only a fraction of him is directly involved in the seeing. Again, many are stimulated, yet only one.

Socrates: Just as the whole planet sees, yet only a fraction of her is directly involved in the seeing! Just as several astronomers are stimulated, but only one Earth! If you're quite complacent about these paradoxes at the human level, it's surely a little absurd to find them so outrageous at the planetary level. In fact they're just what – on the principle of nature's continuity – we should expect there. The discovery that her way of getting to know her companions is in notable ways like a man's way of getting to know his companions does her no harm. On the contrary, it strengthens her case.

Brown: It certainly looks as if the build-up of Earth's experience is no more remarkable than the build-up of yours or mine, Socrates.

Socrates: In this instance at least, Archdeacon, isn't it *less* remarkable? Let me explain. These eyes see a shape, these ears hear a sound, these fingers feel a surface – three unlike instruments registering three unlike objects – yet the result's simply Socrates registering Brown. If such a synthesis at the human level is all right, what's the matter with the much easier synthesis at the planetary level? For Mars is visible only, and not audible or tangible: now it's only a question of compounding *like* impressions. The Professor and Sir Hugo and you see the same Mars – three similar instruments registering one object. Small wonder, then, if the result should be one Earth registering this same object. Certainly it shouldn't shock Dr. Schmidt, who tells us that it isn't the merging but the separation of human minds which is so difficult. Still less should it worry Professor Cowen, who has no time for minds or souls apart from their sense contents. For him, in so far as the contents of our minds are one and the same, our minds are one and the same: one view means one viewer. Observing Mars, we're a single observer, for there's nothing to hold our experience apart.

Brown: That's fine, Socrates, as far as it goes. But think of the bitter struggle among Earth's creatures. How are we to reconcile war and its horrors with her unity?

Socrates: I don't suppose you find any trace, Professor Cowen, in the well-ordered economy of our own bodies, of struggle and ruthlessness and sudden death?

Cowen: I find much more than a trace. If you're looking for law and order in the human body, expect the kind that belongs to the jungle rather than the city. Something like an unremitting struggle among cells and tissues is, in fact, a condition of health. Normally the balance of opposing forces (to change the metaphor) is kept up. When it fails we fall sick.

Socrates: I must say my own experience bears you out. If the history of that republic of organs called Socrates had gone quite smoothly – if head and belly and sex organs had always agreed – would there have been a Socrates, or a man of any sort? It looks as if, up to a point, rivalry and even war among the parts makes for a lively whole.

Cowen: But remember we're talking about organisms, not goddesses!

Socrates: If the 'warfare' within a man is no reason for denying his wholeness or health, neither is the warfare within his planet any reason for denying hers. On the contrary, it seems likely she cannot spare it, and that total pacification might be the death of her. But no doubt the internal strife can be too severe and unbalanced, and then she's diseased.

Brown: I shouldn't call Z-bombs evidence of glowing health! And that brings me, Socrates, to a question I've been wanting to ask you for some time. What are the practical consequences of your doctrine? What do you think would happen if (as you'd say) men came to their senses and discovered their unity – their identity, if you like

– in their living Mother, and in the heavenly beings that rank above her? Do you hold out any hopes of realizing the peace on Earth we so much long for?

Socrates: Bearing in mind what the Professor has just told us, Archdeacon, I should think the hopes are small. The peace *of* Earth is indeed ours whenever, by embracing in understanding and sympathy all her creatures, we care to make it ours. But the peace *on* Earth you speak of is quite another thing, and I suspect no more capable of realization than peace in the human body. It looks to me as if the peace of one level is only to be found at the next: you might say that man *is* the pacification of his cells, and Earth the pacification of men.

Brown: And God the pacification of the universe, the healer of all the world's wounds.

Socrates: Let us then, by every means in our power, seek serenity where serenity belongs – not among the parts but in their whole, not among men but in the divine realm above men. And, having found it there in our dear country, let us bring down to our earthly country as much of it as we are able, and is proper to the troubled scene below. Then at least the strife may be tempered with charity, and the worst catastrophes avoided. And, if man must still fight man, he may give him all honour because he knows that all are one in heaven, and that all his hatred is in the end self-hatred.

Brown: Well, I'm sure of this: the true ground and sanction of human love and mutual forbearance doesn't lie in man as mere man, but in the reality that transcends him, and ultimately in God himself. To lose the divine is to be in terrible danger of losing the human. In defending the one, Socrates is defending the other also.

# FIFTEEN

Cowen: This discussion seems to be deteriorating into a religious service of some kind. Please excuse me from your devotions. Socrates in Wonderland is an amusing fairy-tale up to a point, but when its cleverly sustained nonsense takes on a pious air, I feel slightly revolted. Shall we come down to Earth again – and if possible to earth with a small e?

Canopus: That reminds me of something. I've been wondering whether the real differences between you and Socrates aren't merely verbal ones. If you like to define the Earth as the planet *excluding* her living creatures, and he prefers to define her as the planet *including* her living creatures, why then in the first case she's dead by definition, and in the second she's alive. And that's about all there is to it.

Cowen: Why not end on that more amicable note, Socrates?

Socrates: No doubt Sir Hugo's peace terms are well meant, but any immediate celebrations would, I think, be premature. I take it that useful definitions aren't altogether arbitrary, but have some regard to the facts? Very well. Now at the start of our talk I took Earth to be the mere lodging of the human race, who had arrived from elsewhere. But you, my friends, showed me my mistake, and taught me that her creatures are her own product, her natural elaboration, never for a moment to be parted from her. Am I right?

Canopus: Perfectly right.

Socrates: In that case, Sir Hugo, you must be wrong, and we're all heavily committed to this second definition of Earth – the realistic one – the one you mistakenly attribute to me instead of to the Professor. It's much too late for any of us to go back on it now.

Canopus: I dare say you're right, Socrates. But does it make so much difference, after all, which definition we use – so long as we stick to it?

Socrates: My dear friend, it makes the world of difference! So long as you define the Earth as dead, there's nothing she can do about it: she stays dead. No limb she puts out, no organ she grows, no mind she cultivates, nothing she can do or say will ever persuade you – for the simple reason that it isn't hers. It is alive, and therefore by definition no part of her! Let her show the slightest stirring, the most tentative life-shoot, and at once you mentally amputate it: she's a mere clod, and this life can only be a mere infection of her surface. Look at a man in this way, and he's nothing but a cell-infested skeleton. Examine the liveliest creature in the universe till you know it inside out, and you'll find only a more or less thickly populated terrain. To live is to be torn up by the roots.

You're no longer a terrestrial feature if you can swim, or fly, or walk, or breathe, or grow: these are absolute disqualifications. Is there no way, then, of becoming planetary? Only petrifaction. To rank as a geological specimen you must stop geologizing, stop thinking, stop living, and get yourself buried and thoroughly fossilized: then, if you're unrecognizable enough, you'll belong again. Death and decay are your only pass to Earth. She is dust; and till your dust mingles with hers it is – by the magic of your definition – unearthly, not even star-dust. In short, you're so in love with death that you'll go to any length of self-deception to preserve the world untainted, in the purity of its primeval lifelessness... Clearly, Sir Hugo, an unrealistic definition can in its own way be as lethal as any Z-bomb!

Brown: I suspect they're not unconnected.

Socrates: You do seem to have the knack of putting your ideas into disastrous practice!

Brown: My own impression is that the practice develops naturally out of the theory; and we can scarcely atomize everything but ourselves. Hellish fact follows close on the heels of hellish thinking.

Socrates: Apparently Dr. Schmidt understated the case when he said that cutting yourself off from your past – human and animal and planetary – is a kind of *attempted* suicide. The attempt is apt to come off. But fortunately the downward path to death and hell isn't the only way of becoming planetary again. There is also the path that leads lifewards and heavenwards. If, instead of starting with this mystical definition of Earth – the one which begs the question of her life by ruling it out in advance – we start with the realistic definition – the one which respects all I've learned from you today – then we see her as the great Seed and Root of every flower, the Trunk of every limb, the Thinker even of the thought that denies her.

All this is true, not merely of the Earth, but even more of the Sun and the Galaxy and the great universe itself. The life of the leaf belongs to the trunk no less than to the branch and the twig. And it's you, my dear friends, who've made it impossible to pretend that we leaves are really a flock of migrant birds roosting for the night on the dead and withered boughs of the universe-tree.

# SIXTEEN

Cowen: Anything you say will be taken down by Socrates and misused in evidence against you, or your friends.

Socrates: My dear Professor, there must be some misunderstanding. If I'm a troublesome pupil it's only because of my anxiety to learn. I value your separate lessons so much that I must add them up. Do any of you wish to withdraw anything you've said?

Cowen: For myself, I stand by every word; though I admit if I'd known you as well as I do now, Socrates, I'd have been more guarded. As for my scientific friends here – well, I was startled. I'm no astronomer, Canopus, but...

Canopus: I can't think of anything I want to take back. Of course it's outside my department, but I felt that you and Schmidt went rather far with that business about bodily extensions. In several ways I thought you played into Socrates' hands unnecessarily.

Schmidt: Funnily enough, that is exactly what I was thinking about you two. Once again, my own position is quite clear. I'm concerned with experience, with psychological facts; how far they answer to outside reality is the province of you physical scientists, and I'd rather not trespass in it. What I've said I stick to, though I might have put it more cautiously.

Brown: Off his guard, a man's relatively honest: he's no time to cook up a consistent story.

Socrates: So each expert, while standing by his own contribution, will have nothing to do with the others, and rejects the total altogether. But at the beginning of our conversation you claimed as your one certain accomplishment your science of the universe. In that case – if the word *science* means knowledge and not learned chaos, and the word *universe* means the whole and not fragments – the modern world must have at least a few scientists whose job is to disentangle and gather up the threads of all your separate findings and weave them into an intelligible pattern, into a universe. If even I, who lack every qualification, have nevertheless managed to knit together one or two of your loose ends tonight, what elegant designs – satisfying head and heart alike – will appear when an expert comes to our aid! You really must talk one of them into joining us, Sir Hugo.

Canopus: There's no such person. That sort of synthesis would be more the job of a philosopher than a scientist.

Socrates: The distinction is one I don't seem able to grasp. But never mind about that. Obviously, from what you say, we must get a philosopher to help us.

Brown: As a matter of fact, we did invite a very eminent one to come and meet you, Socrates. To his immense regret he had to decline. It seems there's a conference of modern philosophers going on here.

Socrates: What about?

Brown: I think the topic is 'Language, Philosophy, and Science' – something about the difference between factual and linguistic propositions, as far as I can recollect.

Socrates: By heavens, this is a bit of good news! How necessary, how wisely cautious of your philosophers to whet their verbal tools before using them on the universe. When do you think their preparations will be over, and they'll be ready to make a start?

Brown: Never!

Socrates: What's that?

Brown: I said: never!

Socrates: You're joking.

Brown: I'm perfectly serious. My philosopher friends tell me they aren't concerned with *what* science says about the universe, but with *how* she says it. And, so far as I can make out, they're quite happy to stay that way.

Socrates: I'm sorry to be so dense, but this is beyond my comprehension. It's inconceivable that men who call themselves philosophers – lovers of wisdom – can have no curiosity about the universe and their relationship to it.

Brown: Well, those that have any manage to hide their guilty secret remarkably well.

Canopus: For myself, I must say I find it damping, when I'm trying to interest a philosopher in the stars and galaxies, to find it's my syntax he's got his eye on, and that he's more apt to get excited over the structure of a sentence than the structure of the universe. Not that the situation often arises: he doesn't give me the chance.

Brown: There are a few exceptions, but they are the rogues and vagabonds among philosophers.

Socrates: Rogues? You mean they sell their wisdom, making a living out of it like the Sophists?

Brown: Far from it! I imagine they have difficulty in *giving* it away. Synthesis, cosmology, the philosophy of nature – you'll find such words only in the foul language appendix of the modern philosopher's dictionary. In fact, he's become just as narrow a specialist as the average scientist – a specialist in language, or rather in one aspect of language: definitions and their formal consequences, and that sort of thing.

Socrates: More and more curious. Well, if neither the scientist nor the philosopher can help us out, we seem to be left with the plain man.

Cowen: Who's quite unqualified to give an opinion – supposing he had one.

Socrates: Here's a ripe situation! The findings of the separate sciences can't be reconciled and combined by the scientist, because he's a specialist in only one set of acts; or by the philosopher, because he's a specialist in words and not facts at all; or by the plain man, because he's a specialist in nothing, and neither a scientist nor a philosopher. And so the scientists are quite happy to go on discussing their respective fragments of the universe endlessly, without ever fitting them together into a universe; and the philosophers are quite happy to go on discussing the discussion of the universe endlessly, without ever discussing the universe; and the man-in-the-street is quite happy to go on discussing nothing important at all. The universe can go hang itself. And, by all the gods, that's just about what it *has* done, so far as you're concerned.

Canopus: Come, Socrates, is it quite as bad as all that? We scientists still seem to make a few discoveries, and the philosophers still seem to find plenty to jaw about.

Socrates: For how long? I wonder. The builder who gets so interested in his separate piles of materials that he forgets the house, isn't likely to remain even an efficient collector of materials; and the craftsman who gets so interested in sharpening his tools that he forgets what he was going to use them on, is one day going to find them worn out. I doubt whether it is only your universe that suffers.

Brown: You have every reason to be horrified, Socrates. But remember that fashions change. The universe must one day be rediscovered. The time will come when we shall pay attention to our own science, and no longer leave it to you to begin making sense of it. Meanwhile, the plain fact

of the matter is that you could go on building up a case –
yes, a case a hundred times stronger than the one you've
already built up for a living universe – without beginning
to convert us. It is only through the windows of our lunatic
asylums that you will find modern man looking up at the
living stars. Your fundamental mistake all along has been
to imagine that argument will sway us. Except when it
suits us, we're impervious to reason. The climate of the age
is unhealthy for the gods. It isn't that the modern world
rejects them; it doesn't even consider them. I myself, as a
man of religion, have in theory much respect for your view
and see its reasonableness, but try as I may I can't *actively*
share it.

Socrates: Supposing one of your philosophers had been
eavesdropping on our conversation, what do you suppose
he'd have to say?

Brown: That would depend on how forthright he was.
He might remark that our picture of a living universe is
a kind of poetry; or that he can't understand it; or that he
can't see how it could be verified, and therefore can't attach
any definite meaning to it – three more or less polite ways
of telling us we're talking rot.

Socrates: Never mind: we should be getting somewhere.
I don't know about our poetry or his understanding, but
verification is another matter. I should simply ask him how
he verifies *his* picture of a *dead* universe, and agree heartily

with him as soon as he'd shown me.

Brown: My dear Socrates, can you really be so simple? Isn't it obvious that we're all – philosophers no less than the rest of us – perfectly content to believe blindly in a dead universe without sparing it a second thought, let alone troubling about verification? But supposing by some miracle a few of us turned honest in this matter, and, while suspending final judgment, took our own demand for verification seriously. Then I see a vast and fruitful programme of research opening out – for instance in the fields of large-scale ecology ('the fitness of the environment'), of parapsychology ('a common reservoir of mind'), and of psychology ('levels' of mind linked with 'levels' of nature). To give a particular example: if what thinks matches what is thought about, and astronomers think Earth's thoughts, rather than a mere man's, then planetary psychology – in contrast to the merely human – would need to become a distinct field of empirical study. A vertically organized or hierarchical psychology would not merely explain a lot of things that won't fit into our horizontal or non-hierarchical psychology: it would also suggest a lot of new things to look for. I cannot imagine a more promising hypothesis to work upon.

I could go on indefinitely like this, but what's the use. We have a superstition that the world is dead, and I'm sorry to say there's precious little can be done about it.

Cowen: For a parson – of all people – to accuse anyone of superstition is rather funny. I'm going – I've serious matters to think about. I wish, Socrates, I could stay and explain in detail why your conclusions are all wrong, and your visible gods quite fantastic. But I doubt whether it would make much difference. You're star-struck. In spite of your obviously valiant efforts to bring yourself up to date, it seems you just can't break away from the past, and we're both wasting our time. Anyhow, it's been a great experience meeting you. Goodbye, sir.

Socrates: Goodbye Professor, and thank you for sparing so much of your time. When you feel like sparing a little more – and there's no serious shortage of it in this place – you'll find me here, still eager for instruction.

Canopus: I must be off too. But I'd like you to know, my dear Socrates, that I don't agree with Cowen at all. To say the least, you've shown how an utterly strange world-view can take care of the facts just as well as our familiar one does, if not very much better. By and large, we imagined we'd got the universe taped: evidently we haven't. I think you've made us look pretty silly, and that your visible gods will bear a lot of thinking about. Like the Archdeacon, the main trouble with me is that, though I can follow your argument – all right, I admit it's chiefly *our* argument, with you so effectively in the chair – though I can follow the argument, it carries little conviction. I suspect it's we who are stuck in the mud of our own time, much more than you are in yours. All the same, I'll go on turning these things over in my mind. And perhaps one day, when I'm looking skywards, I shall suddenly be confronted with the blessed gods, alive and shining in heaven after all. Farewell, Socrates: I shall always be proud to count myself your pupil.

# SEVENTEEN

Socrates: Are you leaving us too, Dr. Schmidt?

Schmidt: I'm now off. But before we part, Socrates, there's just one point I'd like to clear up. The Archdeacon here implied that our modern picture of the universe is a mere arbitrary fashion, in today and out tomorrow. It isn't anything of the sort. It's the result of a long and orderly historical process, a psychological development of the utmost importance – as you'd realize at once if you knew the whole story.

Socrates: Do go on.

Schmidt: I'll try to sum it up in a few words. Primitive man was pre-psychological. He didn't feel frightened in a gloomy place: he saw devils there. He didn't feel full of life: he lived in a universe full of life: he saw lively stones and mountains and stars. He didn't think about his dead ancestors: they visited him in dreams. In general, his mind was cosmically distributed, and far more in his stars than his head. What we now call his mental processes were projected on to his world, which was accordingly replete with qualities that appeared to be its own but were really his. Now the progress of civilization and of science is a tale of the slow withdrawal of these projections, in a hundred different ways. One by one these vital and mental attributes leave the surrounding universe for the beholder, thus making genuine knowledge of the world possible. You can't begin to get to grips with ghosts: you can only live in awe of them. The scientist could never anatomize a capricious and life-ridden nature...

Socrates: He has to kill it first! Nor – as we've seen – can he anatomize a capricious and life-ridden man: he has to kill him first. Does that prove he never lived? If science can only investigate a dead universe, then science is no guide to whether the universe is alive or dead.

Schmidt: Would you care to change places with a savage? I don't think you appreciate how ignorant of the world, how fearfully at its mercy, primitive man can be; or how our control of nature demands that we exorcise the spirits that haunt it.

Socrates: To control a wild beast you lock him in a cage, and to control a murderer you chop off his head. But chopping off his head isn't quite the same thing as proving him headless. It's the nature of the universe we're talking about, not how to reverse it.

Schmidt: Speak for yourself, Socrates. I'm not attempting to describe the universe, but only the psychology of the beholder. May I go on?

Let's take, for example, what we might call the psychological history of your Sun god. The tale runs something like this. To our primitive ancestors the Sun is simply alive like you or me, only brighter and more divine. But gradually the animating spirit is distinguished and divided from the body, which becomes a mere ball of fiery matter guided by an independent god or angel. Then science gets under way, and shows that the ball isn't, in fact, steered by particular spirits but by general laws. The Rulers of Nature give place to Rules of Nature, to Tendencies and Forces. And eventually – coming down to our own day – even these ghostly remnants are recognized to be convenient fictions, rather than objective realities presiding over the universe. The stars are no longer guided in their courses. They merely take the path of least resistance. The ball game plays itself.

Socrates: Well, I must say that's a pretty effective way of committing deicide – even if it is a lingering death, spread over many thousands of years! You take the living god, explain that he's really a corpse pushed round by a ghost, and add that you don't believe in ghosts. Fatal results guaranteed! But why confine this treatment to the stars? Haven't you just about as much reason for applying it to man?

Brown: Believe me, Socrates, it *has* been applied to him... But to get back to Dr. Schmidt's celestial murder story: he hasn't completed it. The life has gone, but the body still has to be disposed of. One by one it's sensible qualities are gathered in from the object over there to the subject here. Where are the Sun's colour, his brightness, his warmth? In the perceiver, says science. Even his apparent motion is really ours. Nor are we left with so much as the Sun's bare matter – miserable residue though that is. Our modern physics takes care of that, leaving nothing of him but empty space, practically speaking.

Socrates: A gruesome tale! But what's the sequel? These qualities and life and mind that you've sucked in from your victim the universe – do you find them quite digestible? Is it altogether comfortable to be so full, and your world so empty?

Schmidt: Frankly, no. I believe some disgorging – some re-projection – is needed for our mental health as individuals, and perhaps for the rejuvenation of our culture. That's one reason, Socrates, why I'm so interested in your defence of the visible gods. As a matter of fact, there are already signs of a reversal – mostly among the less educated. Astrology, science-fiction, the flying saucer craze, scores of new-fangled cults on both sides of the Atlantic – all these show that man will not be denied his projections altogether. In fact some religious sects have never withdrawn them to any serious extent. This has its disadvantages, but is on the whole a healthy sign: refusal to project our mental processes on to the world can be very bad for us.

Socrates: I notice you speak with great confidence, Dr. Schmidt, of this projection and withdrawal, this bandying about of life and mind and qualities. No doubt you have some wonderful modern invention, some peculiarly sensitive detector, which enables you to keep track of these remarkable movements in the universe?

Schmidt: You know perfectly well we haven't, Socrates.

Socrates: In that case, how can you tell whether the movements really happen, or only seem to?

Schmidt: They happen all right – as a psychological process, and the psychological evidence is overwhelming. If you want to know where they happen – whether merely in man the perceiver, or at large in the universe, between him and the object – I can't help you. Actually, I think the question is meaningless.

Socrates: But in that case it is meaningless – as well as unhealthy – to maintain that the Sun no longer has the qualities we seem to have deprived him of. And even if he has in fact surrendered them to us, he hasn't lost them. For men also are solar, and members of him. The most that can have happened is that they've shifted from the central part of the Sun or Solar System to the periphery. To go back to your murder story: the murderer turns out to be the organ of his victim, and therefore no murderer at all! Though he has drawn all the life and meaning of this star into his own head, his head (however swelled) still lies within the star (however depleted), and is in fact his chief and most reliable sample of what that star is really like. The entire transaction, the passage of one quality after another from the object over there to the perceiver here, takes place (if at all) inside the living Sun, who suffers no real injury whatever, God bless him! Perhaps it was only his way of dying to live, and getting to know himself better in the process...

Well, all I can say, dear Dr. Schmidt, is that – in spite of yourself – you're his true friend. And mine too. You've completed the case for the visible gods.

Schmidt: It's interesting that you should think so. Well, I must tear myself away: my colleagues are expecting me. If ever you feel like coming along to see us, my dear Socrates, we shall be delighted. Your... your problem is quite fascinating, and I should value the opportunity of going into it one day with you – just the two of us, so that you can talk quite frankly. All this argument we've had today only touches the surface of the problem, doesn't it? It's the hidden motives which matter.

Socrates: Goodbye.

Schmidt: Goodbye Socrates. It's not only been a valuable experience professionally, but also a great personal pleasure to meet you.

# EIGHTEEN

Brown: What an impossible fellow! He's a professional dummy, not a man! At least the others – Canopus and even Cowen – *want* to find out what the world is like, though their efforts (as you've shown so clearly, Socrates) are singularly unsuccessful. But this psychologist just doesn't care: what's worse, he makes a virtue of indifference. And we who do care are lucky if we're not 'interesting cases'. *He's* the case – the one who cries out for his own treatment!

Socrates: Don't be too hard on him, Archdeacon. After all, he's not the only one who will stare at *you* instead of the thing you're pointing at. Some of the most amiable creatures do it – dogs for instance...

Brown: They've some excuse.

Socrates: ...and lovers.

Brown: Yes quite. But the real trouble with this grandly non-committal air of Schmidt's is its dishonesty. It's no more possible to keep up a *neutral* attitude to the universe than to your wife or your supper. These people think it's 'scientific' – 'modern' and 'starkly unsentimental' and all that – to have no opinion about the universe, but what really happens is that their opinion stays unconscious and probably infantile; anyway the very reverse of scientific. This isn't genuine scepticism, for which I've the greatest respect, but either cowardice or laziness – or both. Give me Cowen, who at least has the guts to expose himself to your fire.

Socrates: All the same, Archdeacon, Dr. Schmidt's evidence for the visible gods wouldn't have been half so telling if he'd intended it that way. And the same applies to the other two.

Brown: That's true enough.

Socrates: There's still the question: how far can I take the four of you as typical of your time? Perhaps I've been unlucky.

Brown: The perfectly typical scientist doesn't exist – yet – thank the Lord! And don't dream of judging all parsons by me! We're individual men rather than representative experts; and remember we've been talking off the cuff, among laymen, after an experience that has stirred us up a good deal. In short, you'd have to look a long way before you found four men who'd say exactly what we've said. Even so, Socrates, you can take our general attitude to your living universe as typical of modern educated opinion; if anything, we've been exceptionally kind to it.

Socrates: Now we're alone, Archdeacon, what do you really feel, yourself?

Brown: I'm afraid this is going to take an awful lot of squaring with my Church's teaching! I can hear all sorts of rude words like pantheism, immanentism – not to mention theosophy and worse – being used.

Socrates: That'll never do! Clearly you must trim God's universe to the template of your theology, and if these cosmic beings won't go in, stoutly deny them. That's His fault. He should be more orthodox!

Brown: I deserved that one, Socrates! But seriously what *are* these heavenly creatures? Gods, angels, daemons – no name seems to fit them precisely.

Socrates: And if they are nameless, how can they exist!

Brown: It's not quite true that gods – or angels, or finite superhuman beings of any sort – have dropped out of our modern life altogether. Your visible gods were quietly laid to rest centuries ago, of course, but their ghosts still haunt us. Modern poets have been known to see them. Our stained glass windows and Christmas cards aren't quite the thing without angels. As for us parsons, we're always solemnly – even fervently – announcing their existence and power. To the Founder of our religion, whose words we reverence as truth itself, they were always a vivid reality. All the great surviving religions of the world, and most of the minor ones, insist upon something of the kind. Reason, as you've shown, comes down firmly on their side. And yet...

Socrates: Well?

Brown: And yet the most the modern man of religion can do – if he has any education at all – is half believe. We're bundles of inconsistencies. We babble about a sacramental universe, and then are horrified – or at least mystified – when anyone tries to reunite the material and spiritual worlds. Some of us even pretend that by liquidating the ministers of the court of heaven we are somehow guarding the sovereignty of its Monarch. As if their decline were nothing to do with the decline of religion itself, and with the soul-sickness and despair that accompany that decline!

Socrates: Still you have a sort of heaven left, however depopulated.

Brown: Not one heaven, Socrates, but two; and between them there's no bridge. The heavens of the theologian and the astronomer have drifted so far apart that neither throws the least light upon the other, and even their languages are different. There's no chance at all of the Archbishop of Canterbury and the Astronomer Royal putting their heads together to draw a composite picture of heaven.

Socrates: Or rather, to *redraw* it.

Brown: Precisely: their heavens weren't always so incongruous. More than one of the great Early Fathers of the Church taught that the Sun and stars are rational and moral creatures. In any case the historical debt that our religion owes to the pre-Christian cults of the Sun-god and the Great Mother is quite incalculable. And even now the divorce of the visible Sun from all its spiritual connotations isn't quite complete. For some of our own children – as for vast numbers of our Christian ancestors –

there exists only one heaven: a heaven (to use your words) at once astronomical and theological. At any rate when I was a child I believed that the angels shared the sky with the stars, diving and soaring overhead like religious birds of paradise in God's aviary. I sang hymns about a heaven 'above the bright blue sky', and was encouraged to take the gospel story of the Ascension on trust, just as it stands. If heaven lay about me in my infancy, its general direction was upwards.

Socrates: But you were soon made aware of your childish mistake, I don't doubt.

Brown: All too soon. I was warned that though the heavens may declare the mathematics of God, for his glory I must look elsewhere – or rather, nowhere, in no place at all. I was informed that when Dante populated the spheres of the Moon and planets and stars with the blessed – the higher the sphere the more excellent – he was writing poetic nonsense. So was Shakespeare, in those lovely lines about the orbs 'still quiring to the young-ey'd cherubims'. So again, was your great disciple Plato, and Plotinus, and all the other ancients who in rapturous language described the stars as immortal and happy gods, and their motion as the grand dance and procession of the universe. So was the author of the book of Job, when he said that 'the morning stars sang together, and the sons of the gods shouted for joy'.

Socrates: Call it literature, and there's no danger of anybody taking it seriously!

Brown: Not the slightest! All such ecstatic talk about the heavens above we now realise to be nothing but beautiful white lies, so patently false that nobody bothers to refute them. The founders of our civilization might believe they lived in a world which grew more and more lively and intelligent and divine as you worked out from Earth and man at the centre; and now we, their heirs, are sure the world is arranged the other way about. Modern man has not only turned his garment the universe inside out, but imagines this is the only way it can be worn. Now when we look up at the stars we see nothing but so many tons of superheated material, or something like a badly organized fireworks display in slow motion – instead of the dear country we came from and hope to go back to. Your living stars aren't merely stone dead and buried in the unconsecrated ground of the space-time continuum, but decayed almost beyond recognition. To us, your ancient wisdom of the skies is at its best so much charming but infantile folly, and at its worst raving madness.

Socrates: And you have today explained your reasons?

Brown: My dear Socrates, you've seen we have *no* reasons! We *know*, that's all. You're not dealing with rational people, but with devotees of a cult – a religion masquerading in scientific get-up. It's always difficult to argue with the devout, but when they take their beliefs about the universe so much for granted that they think they've no beliefs at all, then your task is almost hopeless. And the crowning joke is, of course, that it is *we* – of all people – who've found the solid scientific reasons for believing in the sort of universe that you believed in on instinct! It is *we* (as you've made us admit) who've confirmed and completed the ancient vision of a tremendously living universe – and we've done so without disturbing in the least our crypto-religious belief in the very opposite thing!

In short, my dear Socrates, I can't imagine what you think of us – except that our capacity for self-deception and double-thinking – our hypocrisy if you like – is unbounded!

Socrates: Well, my very dear Archdeacon, at least I've never met a more honest hypocrite than you – whatever an honest hypocrite can be! I think you'll soon wake up to find yourself on the right side of Heaven's door – the Heaven you've been in all the while without knowing it! And now I shall bid you goodbye with great affection, and go out to see which of the bright gods are visible tonight. Perhaps – who knows? – they'll throw some ray of light on that wonderful thing – the mind of modern man!

www.ingramcontent.com/pod-product-compliance
Lightning Source LLC
Chambersburg PA
CBHW020905090426
42736CB00008B/505